W9-BNF-147

SELECTED LEGAL ISSUES IN CATHOLIC SCHOOLS

Sr. Mary Angela
Shaughnessy,
SCN, J.D., Ph.D.

BISHOP MUELLER LIBRARY
Briar Cliff College
SIOUX CITY, IA 51104

Secondary Schools Department
National Catholic Educational Association

Copyright ©1998 National Catholic Educational Association
1077 30th Street, NW; Washington, DC 20007-3852

ISBN 1-55833-209-X

39979675

DEDICATION

I dedicate this work to my brother,

Edward M. Shaughnessy, III,

a man who gives his life in the service of others.

He is truly the wind beneath his family's wings,

and my hero.

In gratitude, your sister,

Angie

TABLE OF
CONTENTS

FOREWORD

Sr. Mary Angela Shaughnessy has been a unique and wonderful asset to Catholic educators for years. To say she is prolific would be an understatement. Her list of publications may put her second only to the legendary Andrew Greeley, and she has yet to try her hand at fiction.

We asked Sr. Mary Angela if she would be willing to prepare a manuscript that would look carefully at legal issues that are especially important for Catholic high schools. Since her productivity is as much a reflection of her generosity as it is her competence, she agreed, hence this publication.

As befits a review of legal issues, a few initial caveats may be in order. While this text offers analysis, recommendations and examples that are particularly useful to Catholic high schools, most of the principles of law that are cited are applicable to all Catholic schools, and indeed to all private schools. Much of chapter two reviews aspects of tort law that apply to virtually all schools, public and private. For better or worse, the legal content in which Catholic secondary schools function is neither simple or unique.

Secondly, as Sr. Mary Angela reminds her readers often, civil law does not define the full range of the Catholic school's responsibilities to fairness and justice. She offers important distinctions between what civil law permits and demands, and what should constitute good and honorable practice in a Catholic school. These distinctions may make her text less interesting to some, but they also make this a book we are proud to publish.

Michael J. Guerra
Executive Director
Secondary Schools Department

Feast of St. Joseph 1998

PREFACE

It is my hope that this text will provide both information and a process for shared reflection. Each chapter is followed by questions for discussion.

It has been my privilege to research, write, and speak on the topic of law and Catholic schools for approximately the last fourteen years. My travels across the United States and abroad have put me in touch with many inspiring, committed Catholic educators. As a former Catholic high school principal and teacher, I have experienced the joy-filled, but demanding, ministry of Catholic secondary education. I would like to thank all those who have shared that ministry with me.

I am also grateful to my religious community, the Sisters of Charity of Nazareth, and its leadership for giving me the opportunities and education to minister in Catholic education. I wish to express my particular gratitude to women who served in leadership roles while I have been a member of the community, particularly Mother Lucille Russell, Sister Barbara Thomas, Sister Dorothy MacDougall, Sister Emily Nabholz, and Sister Elizabeth Wendeln.

I express gratitude to friends and colleagues at Spalding University in Louisville, Kentucky, where I am privileged to serve. I must especially thank the President of Spalding University, Dr. Thomas R. Oates, whose support and encouragement have enabled me to continue in this work. He is a true Catholic educator whose belief in Catholic secondary education has been especially embodied in Spalding's assuming ownership of two Catholic high schools so that their survival and growth would be ensured.

Many thanks to my beloved sister and friend, Janet Kellogg, who worked diligently as typist of this manuscript. The support of other family members helps sustain me as well.

I thank Mr. Michael Guerra, Executive Director of NCEA's Secondary Department, for his support and encouragement of all my work, and especially this text.

Lastly, I thank all of you who may read this text. I pray that it may help make the law a more Gospel-based reality and a practical compass for your day-to-day work with young people. May God bless you.

Mary Angela Shaughnessy, SCN, J.D., Ph.D.
January, 1998

CHAPTER ONE

SOURCES OF THE LAW

Fairness and due process

Federal and state statutes

Guidelines

For Reflection and Discussion

CHAPTER ONE

SOURCES OF THE LAW

Constitutional law is one of the major components of civil law in the United States today and is the main source of the law for the public school. In the majority of public school student and teacher dismissal cases, plaintiffs allege deprivation of constitutional rights.

Catholic educators are probably familiar with certain constitutional rights. The First Amendment guarantees freedom of speech, press, assembly, and religion; the Fourth Amendment protects against unlawful searches and seizures; the Fifth and Fourteenth Amendments guarantee due process.

Public school teachers and students, of course, can claim constitutional rights because the public school is a government agency, and those who administer public schools are government agents. The Constitution protects persons from arbitrary governmental deprivation of their constitutional freedoms. Persons in Catholic schools, however, cannot claim such protections because Catholic schools are private institutions administered by private persons.

These restrictions may seem unfair, yet a similar price is paid by anyone who works in a private institution. If a person goes to work in a supermarket, the person will probably be required to wear a uniform. The employee will not be permitted to wear a button advertising a different supermarket chain. First Amendment protections do not exist for supermarket employees.

The bottom line is that when one enters a private institution such as a Catholic school, one voluntarily surrenders the protections of the Constitution. A Catholic school teacher or student can always leave the Catholic school, but so long as the person remains in the institution, constitutional protections are not available. Thus, the Catholic school does not have to accept behaviors about which the public school has no choice, and even is required to protect.

What cannot lawfully be done in a public school may be done in a Catholic school. As stated earlier, the First Amendment to the Constitution protects persons' rights to free speech; therefore, administrators in public schools may not make rules prohibiting the expression of an unpopular viewpoint.

Most educators have heard of the landmark *Tinker* case which produced the now famous line, "Neither students or teachers shed their constitutional rights at the [public] schoolhouse gate." Since no such constitutional protection exists in the Catholic school, administrators may restrict the speech of both students and teachers.

Fairness and due process

Public schools must be concerned with constitutional issues. Catholic schools, while not bound to grant constitutional freedoms per se, are bound to act in a manner characterized by fairness. Some legal experts talk about a "smell" test. If an action "smells" wrong when a person examines it, it may be suspect. In the end, the actions expected of Catholic schools may appear much like constitutional protections. In no area is this more evident than in due process considerations.

The Fifth Amendment to the Constitution guarantees the federal government will not deprive someone of "life, liberty, or property without due process of law." The Fourteenth Amendment made the Fifth Amendment and all other amendments in the Bill of Rights applicable to the states.

Persons entitled to constitutional due process have substantive due process rights, property interests (that which can be the subject of ownership, including jobs and education) and liberty interests (freedom, reputation). Substantive due process involves moral as well as legal ramifications: Is this action fair and reasonable? Substantive due process applies whenever property or liberty interests can be shown.

The Constitution also guarantees procedural due process, *how* a deprivation occurs. In the public school, procedural due process includes *notice* (a presentation of the allegations against the accused); *hearing* (an opportunity to respond) *before an impartial tribunal;* opportunity to *confront* and *cross-examine* accusers; and the opportunity to call *witnesses in one's own behalf.* In serious disciplinary cases, a person in the public school has the right to have an attorney present.

Procedural due process has been defined as a question: What process is due? In the public sector, several elements are present. In meeting the requirements of fairness, Catholic school educators should ask themselves these questions:

- What are our disciplinary procedures?
- Are they reasonable?
- Are all students treated fairly and, as far as reasonably possible, in the same way?
- Are there clear procedures that students and parents can expect will be followed?

Catholic schools, while not bound to provide the whole panoply of procedural due process protections that public schools must provide, are nonetheless expected to be fair. An Ohio court, ruling in a Catholic school discipline case, stated that courts could intervene in private school disciplinary cases, if "the proceedings do not comport with fundamental fairness" *(Geraci v. St. Xavier High School)*. Fundamental fairness in a Catholic school is akin to, but not synonymous with, constitutional due process in the public school.

Federal and state statutes

Federal and state statutes and regulations, many of which reflect theories of constitutional law, comprise a second source of the law affecting Catholic schools and their personnel. If a statute requires that all who operate an educational institution within a given state follow a certain directive, both Catholic and public schools are bound. So long as what is required does not unfairly impinge upon the rights of Catholic schools and can be shown to have some legitimate educational purpose, Catholic schools can be compelled to comply with state legislative requirements.

The only situation in which a Catholic school can be required to grant federal constitutional protections occurs when state action can be found to be so pervasive within the school that the school can fairly be said to be acting as an agent of an individual state. The key factor in state action is the nexus or relationship between the state and the challenged activity. Although litigants have alleged state action in Catholic schools, no court of record has found state action present in private school teacher or student dismissal cases.

In a 1982 teacher dismissal case, *Rendell-Baker v. Kohn*, the Supreme Court ruled that a dismissal from a private school which received 90-99% of its funding from the state did not constitute state action. *Rendell-Baker* seems to render the state action issue moot in cases alleging violation of constitutional due process protections. A different situation can exist in cases alleging violations of federal anti-discrimination and civil rights legislation. In those cases, the presence of federal funding can result in an institution's being required to abide by the legislation.

Since Catholic schools are not bound to grant constitutional protections unless significant state action is found, litigants alleging a denial of constitutional due process will have to prove the existence of significant state action within the institution before the court will grant relief. It is very important for Catholic school educators to keep these facts in mind.

It is not uncommon for parents, students or teachers to claim that their constitutional rights have been violated in the Catholic school when, in fact, no constitutional rights ever existed in the first place. These realities need to be clarified very early in a relationship between a Catholic school and its staff, students and parents. One way to prevent possible misunderstandings is to develop and disseminate comprehensive handbooks which outline the rights and responsibilities of all persons in the Catholic school.

Guidelines

The beginning point for rules development should be the school's philosophy and mission. All students can be brought to some understanding of institutional philosophy: "At our school we try to treat each other the way Jesus would." The life of the school should be seen as flowing from its philosophy.

Rules should be clear and understandable. The test that might be applied by the court is: Would two persons of average intelligence reading this rule have the same understanding of it? A rule stating "Students arriving at class after the bell will be marked tardy" is clear, while a rule such as "Late students will be marked tardy" is open to such questions as: How late is late? After the bell? After the teacher begins class?

Whenever possible, rules should be written. It is easier to refer to the written rule when emotions run high than to insist that "at the beginning of the school year this rule was announced."

Courts look for evidence of good faith: Did the institution have a rule promulgated? Did the student know of the rule? The court does not concern itself with the wisdom of the rule—or even with the rightness or wrongness of the professional opinion of educators; the court is only concerned with the existence of a properly promulgated rule and with the institution's acting in good faith according to state procedures. Courts look for basic fairness in the execution of the contract existing between the student/parent and the school, when the student/parent alleges that a school acted improperly.

Educators must understand that it is impossible to identify everything a student might do that could result in discipline, including suspension or expulsion. Therefore, it is advisable to have some kind of " catch-all" clause such as "other inappropriate conduct" or "conduct, whether inside or outside the school, that is detrimental to the reputation of the school." No court will expect a school to have listed all possible offenses, but courts will expect that there are written rules and that students and parents have a reasonable idea of the expectations of the school.

Every school should have some written handbook. Parents should be required to sign a form stating that they have read the rules and agree to be governed by them. Handbooks are discussed in greater detail in Chapter Fourteen.

When considering the development of student guidelines, educators should be aware that there is a time investment involved. If a teacher allows a student to tell his or her story instead of summarily imposing punishment ("All students whose names are on the board will remain after school"), the teacher makes a commitment to spending time with a student who faces discipline. The principal or disciplinarian makes a commitment to listening to the student's side of the story as well as to the teacher's, but the benefit should be obvious: students perceive teachers and administrators as trying to be fair and, hopefully, will internalize the values modeled.

Somewhat more extensive procedures should be developed if the penalty is suspension. One-day suspensions, at minimum, require that the principal or vice-principal be involved and that the parents be notified. Longer suspensions should involve a written notice of the charges and a hearing.

Cases in which the possibility of expulsion exists require both formal notification and a hearing at which the student normally should be able to confront accusers. Careful documentation must be kept in all major disciplinary proceedings. There is no requirement, however, that a student be allowed to have legal counsel present at any stage of the Catholic school's disciplinary proceedings. The guiding principle in any consideration of student rights and discipline should be the desire to act in a Christian manner characterized by fairness and compassion.

For Reflection and Discussion

- Student C is angry with you for giving her a detention because she was wearing an article of clothing in violation of the dress code and/or uniform rules. She tells you that she has a First Amendment right to freedom of expression. How will you respond?

- Student K has asked you at the beginning of class, "So, do we have any rights in a Catholic school?" What will you say?

TORT LAW: FOR WHAT ARE EDUCATORS LIABLE?

Corporal punishment

Search and seizure

Defamation of character

Negligence

For Reflection and Discussion

TORT LAW: FOR WHAT ARE EDUCATORS LIABLE?

Tort cases are the most common form of lawsuit against educators. A tort is a civil or private wrong other than a breach of contract. The four main types of tort cases found in schools are: corporal punishment, search and seizure, defamation of character, and negligence. Negligence suits outnumber the other three types together. Some of these topics are also considered in other chapters.

Corporal punishment

Although some states permit corporal punishment, Catholic schools would be well advised to avoid it. While the administration of the punishment might not be illegal, injuring the child physically, mentally or psychologically is. The risks of student harm and educator liability make corporal punishment a poor disciplinary choice. High school teachers may believe that corporal punishment is not a problem. However, the definition is much broader than it might appear. Corporal punishment has been defined as any touching that can be construed as punitive. Thus, a teacher must consider how physical contact may be perceived.

Search and seizure

The 1985 Supreme Court decision of *New Jersey v. T.L.O.*, holding that public school officials must use reasonable cause in searching students or their possessions, does not apply to Catholic schools. Catholic schools should, nonetheless, have some kind of policy for searching students and/or seizing their possessions. Searching a student should require "more" cause than searching a student's locker.

Catholic schools can be subject to tort suits of assault and battery and/or invasion of privacy if a student is harmed because of an unreasonable search. Carefully developed policies should guide any search and seizure. A common sense "balancing test" should be applied in each case: Is this search and its possible effect worth finding whatever it is that school officials are seeking?

Defamation of character

Defamation is an unprivileged communication that harms the reputation of another. Defamation can be either spoken (slander) or written (libel). Truth may *not* be an absolute defense for an educator, who is generally held to a higher standard than the ordinary person. Defamation is discussed in greater detail in later chapters. A good rule is: whatever is written must be specific, behaviorally-oriented and verifiable. Catholic schools can protect themselves and their students and teachers by ensuring record-keeping policies are in place that:
1) limit contents of records to what is absolutely necessary,
2) provide for periodic culling of older records, and
3) limit access to records to persons who have legitimate reasons for reading them.

Negligence

If a principal or teacher is sued, the odds are that the suit will allege negligence. Since negligence is an unintentional act which results in injury, a person charged with negligence is generally not going to face criminal charges. Persons who bring successful negligence suits are usually awarded money damages in an amount calculated to compensate for the actual injury suffered. It is possible, though rare, for a court to award punitive or exemplary damages if the court is shocked by the negligent behavior. There are four elements which must be present before legal negligence can be found:
- *duty,*
- *violation of duty,*

- *proximate cause,* and
- *injury.*

The person charged with negligence must have had a *duty* in the situation. Educators are not responsible for injuries occurring at a place where, or at a time when, they had no responsibility. A principal or teacher, walking through a mall on a weekend, does not have a legal duty to students who are also walking through the mall. Within the school setting, students have a right to safety and teachers and administrators have a duty to protect the safety of all those entrusted to their care. Teachers have a duty to provide reasonable supervision of students. Administrators have a duty to develop and implement rules and regulations guiding teachers in providing for student safety.

Negligence cannot exist if the second element, *violation of duty,* is not present. Courts understand that accidents and spontaneous actions can occur. If a teacher is properly supervising a playground and one child picks up a rock and throws it and so injures another child, the teacher cannot be held liable. However, if a teacher who is responsible for the supervision were to allow rock throwing to continue without attempting to stop it and students were injured, the teacher would probably be found to have violated a duty.

Similarly, a teacher who leaves a classroom unattended in order to take a coffee break will generally be found to have violated a duty if a student is injured, and evidence suggests that the teacher's presence could have prevented the injury. If it can be shown that teachers often left students unattended while the principal, through inaction or inattention, did nothing about the situation, the principal has violated a duty as well. Under the legal doctrine of *respondent superior* (let the superior answer), principals are often held responsible for the actions of subordinates.

The violation of duty must be the *proximate cause* of the injury. The court or jury has to decide whether proper supervision could have prevented the injury and, in so deciding, the court has to look at the facts of each individual case. A cause can be proximate, but not direct. If a teacher leaves a class unattended without good reason and one student pokes a pencil in another student's arm, the teacher's lack of supervision could be the proximate cause of the injury even though another student's actions were the direct cause.

The tragic case of *Levandoski v. Jackson City School District,* illustrates this point. A teacher failed to report that a 13-year-old girl was missing from class. The child was later found murdered. The child's mother filed suit against the school district and alleged that if the child's absence had been reported, the murder would not have happened. The court found that no evidence existed proving a causal link between the violation of duty and the injury. Thus, the case failed in proximate cause.

One can easily see how a slight change in the facts could produce a different ruling. Had the child been found dead on or near school property, a court might well have found that proximate cause existed. It is not the act itself which results in legal negligence; it is the causal relationship between the act and the injury. If the relationship is too remote, legal negligence will not be found. Any reasonable educator will try to be as careful as possible, of course, and not gamble on the "causal connection."

A well-known case which illustrates the concept of proximate cause is *Smith v. Archbishop of St. Louis.* A second-grade teacher kept a lighted candle on her desk every morning during May. She gave no special instructions to the students regarding the dangers of lighted candles. One day a child, wearing a crepe paper costume for a school play, moved too close to the candle and the costume caught fire. The teacher had difficulty putting out the flames and the child sustained serious physical and resultant psychological injuries. The trial court ruled that the teacher was the proximate cause of the child's injuries. The court also discussed the concept of *foreseeability*: it was not necessary that the defendant have foreseen the particular injury but only that a reasonable person should have foreseen that some injury was likely.

This discussion should indicate that proximate cause is a complex subject. It is difficult to predict what a court will determine to be the proximate cause in any particular allegation of negligence.

The fourth element necessary for a finding of negligence is *injury*. No matter how irresponsible the behavior of a teacher or administrator, there is no legal negligence if there is no injury. If a teacher leaves 20 first-graders unattended and no one is injured, there is no negligence in a legal sense. In order to bring suit in a court of law, an individual has to have sustained an injury for which the court can award a remedy.

Courts follow the principle, "the younger the child, chronologically or mentally, the greater the standard of care." It might be acceptable to leave a group of high school seniors alone for 10 minutes when it would not be acceptable to leave a group of first-graders alone.

In developing and implementing policies for supervision, the educator must ask, "Is this what one would expect a reasonable person in a similar situation to do?" The best defense for an administrator in a negligence suit is a reasonable attempt to provide for the safety of all through appropriate rules and regulations. The best defense for a teacher is a reasonable effort to implement rules and regulations.

For Reflection and Discussion

- While you are teaching a class, two students appear and tell you that Student B has somehow gotten his hand stuck in the ice cream machine in the student lounge. No other teachers or staff members are nearby. You have twenty-five students in your class, and no way to contact the office. What will you do?

- You supervised a student trip to a nursing home. One student was visiting an elderly couple who had a large window; the student opened the window and attempted to jump to his death. He landed in a gutter where he was eventually rescued by firefighters, but he sustained a broken ankle from the attempt. His parents are talking about suing you on the grounds that you should have foreseen this type of injury and taken plans to avoid it. What do you think—are you negligent or not?

CHAPTER THREE

STUDENT PRIVACY AND REPUTATION: BALANCING RIGHTS WHILE AVOIDING HARM

Defamation of character

Confidentiality of records

For Reflection and Discussion

CHAPTER THREE

STUDENT PRIVACY AND REPUTATION: BALANCING RIGHTS WHILE AVOIDING HARM

P rivacy and reputation are two serious legal issues facing Catholic educators today. Both students and teachers expect that information concerning them will be revealed only to those with a right to know. School officials who fail to take reasonable measures to safeguard such information could face civil lawsuits for defamation of character.

Defamation of character

As stated in the previous chapter, defamation is an unprivileged communication that harms the reputation of another. Defamation, which may involve invasion of privacy, can be either spoken, *slander*, or written, *libel*.

Educators should be concerned with protecting the reputations of all in their schools. Educators should exercise great care in keeping student and teacher records, as well as in speaking about student behavior. It is only just that an educator refrain from gossip or unnecessary derogatory remarks about other teachers and/or students. The best advice for Catholic educators is to be as factual as possible in official documents and to refrain from "editorial" comments. Whatever is written should meet the following three criteria:

1) it should be specific,
2) it should be behaviorally-oriented and
3) it should be verifiable.

It is more professional, and legally more appropriate, to write, "Bobby has been absent four times this month, late for class eight times, and sent to the principal's office for fighting five times," than to write "Bobby is absent too much, late most of the time, and always in trouble." It is better to write, "Susan is reading on a first-grade level" than to write, "Susan can't read."

If there is no reason to have an item in a student's file, it should be stored elsewhere. Disciplinary records, in particular, should not be stored in official files. Students are still in a formative stage, and school officials should exercise extreme caution in storing information that could be harmful to a student. Disciplinary records should not be a part of the information sent to another school when a student transfers or graduates. If the new school requires disciplinary information, the transferring school should consider preparing a document containing the information and having the parents sign a statement that they have seen the document and agree to its being sent.

In today's litigious society, most educators are familiar with the problems of writing legally non-controversial recommendations for students without sacrificing the truth. Further, most teachers have read recommendations that seem to say very little. All educators must understand that no one has an absolute, legal right to a recommendation, however, fairness would seem to indicate that only the most extreme situations should result in a student being denied a recommendation.

College recommendations pose particular problems. For example, a student or parent may demand a recommendation from a certain teacher if the recommendation must come from a teacher in a given discipline. If a teacher were to decline to write the recommendation, the parent would probably simply complain to the principal and/or guidance department head and the teacher may become involved in a battle. Therefore, the following approach is recommended when writing recommendations for students who cannot be recommended.

Students can be given letters verifying enrollment and factual statements can be made about education and participation in extra-curricular activities. The guideline is to be as fair as possible. School officials should strive to be fair and respectful of the dignity of others in all communications, whether official or not, and to say only what can be shown to have some valid relationship to the professional situation. In so doing, school officials protect themselves against possible lawsuits alleging defamation and/or invasion of privacy.

Secondary school teachers may presume that a waiver of the right to read a transcript is absolute, but it is not. Such a waiver is only as good as the custodian of the records. It is not unheard of for a student or parent to contact a college office and ask why a student was not admitted, and be read the recommendation. A teacher can always argue that this is his or her honest opinion, as well it may be. The above mentioned procedures should help, though, in fairly and compassionately attempting to meet students' needs without compromising fairness.

Confidentiality of records

An issue related to invasion of privacy is confidentiality of records. If an educator follows the procedures outlined above, the risk of having problematic materials in student files is minimized.

The contents of student files should be released only to authorized persons. Even faculty and staff should be given access to student files only for appropriate, school-related reasons. Parental signatures should be required before records are sent to anyone.

Many educators in Catholic schools can recall when neither they nor students' parents were permitted access to their student records. In 1975 the Buckley Amendment, granting students and parents the right to inspect school records, was passed by Congress. It must be frankly stated that there are some legal experts who believe that the Buckley Amendment does not apply to private schools. The amendment contains a clause which provides that the legislation does not apply to private schools *solely* because of the presence of government funds (e.g., federal commodities in cafeterias, bloc grant money, etc.). However, this belief has never been tested in court.

There are cases in which private sector officials have been required to comply with federal legislation, such as anti-discrimination statutes. The requirement was based on public policy considerations, commonly accepted standards of behavior. It is better to comply *voluntarily* with legislation such as the Buckley Amendment than to risk becoming a test case for the courts. Legalities aside, it seems only right that persons affected by records have the right to see them.

For Reflection and Discussion

- Student Y, who has a D average in your class, asks you to write a recommendation for her to a highly competitive college. You believe she has virtually no chance of success. How will you respond? Will you write the recommendation?

CHAPTER FOUR

STAFF/STUDENT RELATIONSHIPS

Confidentiality

Sexual misconduct

Other physical contact

Other behaviors

For Reflection and Discussion

CHAPTER FOUR

STAFF/ STUDENT RELATIONSHIPS

Teachers and other staff members care about students. That care extends to all areas of student life. Educators often find themselves counseling students in personal matters; it is not unusual for a teacher to find him/herself in the position of "surrogate parent." Students often entrust teachers with confidential information. Teachers, many with little training in professional counseling, often question what is appropriate in interacting with students outside the classroom setting.

Few guidelines are available. Teachers and other personnel often deal with situations that pose personal and legal risks for the adults as well as for the students. This author is familiar with several situations in which parents threatened and/or pursued legal action against a teacher whose actions they viewed as unwise, inappropriate, sexually motivated or interfering with the parent/ child relationship. All adults working in the educational ministry of the church should be aware of the legal ramifications involved in student/staff relationships, and be careful to avoid the perception as well as the reality of inappropriateness.

Confidentiality

Most educators rightfully consider student confidences sacred. If a student confides in a teacher, the student should be able to presume that the confidential information normally will not be shared with anyone. Educators may believe that they have some type of immunity which protects them from legal liability if they refuse to share student information given in confidence.

However, the facts indicate that very few states provide any sort of immunity or privilege for teachers who receive confidential information from students. If a teacher were subpoenaed, placed on the stand, and asked for confidential information, most judges would require the teacher to answer. The teacher does not enjoy the type of privilege that lawyers and priests have. Chapter Five will provide additional information.

Sexual misconduct

One end of the student/staff relationship spectrum is represented by sexual misconduct. Sexual misconduct *can* be alleged in apparently innocent situations. Students *can* misinterpret touching, and a teacher *could* find him/herself facing child abuse charges. Extreme caution is in order whenever a teacher touches a student.

Another kind of problem is posed by a student who believes that a teacher has not responded to efforts to achieve a closer relationship. Such a student may accuse a teacher of inappropriate conduct as a retaliatory measure. Educators must be aware that serious consequences can result from an allegation of child abuse, even if that allegation is eventually proven to be false. At the very least, such a false allegation can be extremely embarrassing for the teacher. If a child abuse report is made, the teacher will be questioned by authorities and the investigation will be recorded. In some states, lists of suspected child abusers are kept.

Thus, it is imperative that educators protect themselves and the students they teach by practicing appropriate behavior with students. To avoid even the slightest hint of impropriety, a teacher should avoid being alone with a single student behind closed doors unless a window or other opening permits outsiders to see into the area. A good question to ask oneself might be: If this were my child, would I have any objection to a teacher relating with him or her in this manner?

Fear of teachers facing child abuse allegations has caused some public school districts in this country to adopt rules that prohibit any faculty touching of students. Such rules preclude putting one's arm around students, patting a student on the back, and giving a student a hug. No Catholic school educator would want to take such a position, but common sense precautions must be taken for the protection of all.

Other physical contact

Educators can also be charged with child abuse that is not sexual. Corporal punishment, prohibited by regulation in most Catholic schools, can set the stage for allegations of physical abuse. An example of punitive touching occurred when a teacher tapped a child on the shoulder with a folder while reprimanding the child for not having done his homework. The child's mother filed a child abuse report against the teacher and threatened to file charges of assault and battery. Although the case is outrageous, it does indicate the dangers that can exist. Thus, educators are well-advised to adopt the operating rule: Never touch a child in a way that can be construed as punitive. Discussion of this topic can be found in Chapter Two.

Other behaviors

Teachers and other staff members must bear in mind that they are professionals rendering a service. Just as a counselor or psychiatrist is professionally bound to avoid emotional involvement with a client, a teacher should strive to avoid becoming so emotionally involved with a student that objectivity and fairness are compromised. Teachers must remember that they have many students for whom they are responsible and who need and may desire the teacher's attention. If a relationship with a student keeps a teacher from responding to other student needs on a regular basis, the teacher should seriously examine the appropriateness of the relationship.

In seeking to assess the appropriateness of a teacher/student relationship, some mental health professionals recommend asking oneself questions such as these: Whose needs are being met? Is there a boundary? Where is it?

The following adult behaviors could be considered inappropriate, depending on the totality of the circumstances: dropping by a student's home, particularly if no parent is present; frequent telephoning of the student; social trips with a student; sharing of teacher's personal problems.

Serving as a Catholic educator in these times is a privilege and a gift. It is indeed sad when an educator is forced to relinquish that gift because of inappropriate choices. Reflection and prudent behavior will keep educators both legally protected and professionally fulfilled.

For Reflection and Discussion

- Student X, a member of the opposite sex, has been leaving little boyfriend/girlfriend cards on your desk and signing them "With all my heart and all my love." How will you respond?

- You are particularly concerned with the well-being of Student Z who appears to be ill-clothed and under-nourished. He appears at the door of your home around 10 P.M. one evening. He wears only pajamas and says his father has thrown him out. He asks if he can stay with you. What would you answer?

CHAPTER FIVE

KEEPING STUDENT CONFIDENCES: WHAT CAN YOU TELL? WHAT MUST YOU TELL?

Confidentiality

Legal immunity

Journal writing

Retreats

Case law

For Reflection and Discussion

CHAPTER FIVE

KEEPING STUDENT CONFIDENCES: WHAT CAN YOU TELL? WHAT MUST YOU TELL?

One of the more perplexing situations facing Catholic educators today is that presented by student sharing of confidential information. Today's young persons may well face more pressures and problems than young persons of any other decade. Broken homes, alcoholism and drug addiction, sexual and physical abuse, depression, and violence were certainly found in earlier eras, but they seem to be more prevalent, or at least more openly acknowledged, than they were when the majority of Catholic educators were students. The responsibility for receiving student confidences and advising students in both day-to-day situations and crises can be overwhelming. Busy teachers may well ask, "What am I supposed to do? I know I'm not a professional counselor, a psychiatrist, or a social worker but I'm the one the student trusts, the one the student has consulted." Are there certain legal issues involved in the receiving of student confidences? Are there matters that must be made known to others, even when the student has asked for and received a promise of confidentiality?

These are good questions for any educator to ask. Teachers cannot afford to think that they can help all students all the time.

It is not possible. If a student were to come to a teacher and tell the teacher he or she is experiencing shortness of breath and chest pain, the teacher would quickly summon both the student's parents and medical assistance. Yet, psychological problems are no less serious than physical ones, and the layperson who attempts to deal with such problems unaided may well be courting tragedy for both self and student.

Confidentiality

Confidentiality is generally held to mean that one individual or individuals will keep private information that has been given to them, and will not reveal it. For example, the person who receives the sacrament of reconciliation rightfully expects that the subject matter of confession will be held sacred by the confessor and will not be revealed to anyone. Indeed, there are accounts of priests who died rather than break the seal of confession.

Friends share confidences with each other. One individual may say to another, "This is confidential. You cannot repeat it." The person speaking in confidence has a right to expect that the confidant to whom the information has been given will keep the matter confidential. But there are recognized limits to what friends will keep confidential. If one's friend confides that she has been stockpiling sleeping medication and plans to take all of it that evening so as to commit suicide, it is not hard to see that morality demands that the confidant communicate that knowledge to a spouse or other family member of the confiding individual, or take some other action that would intervene in the attempted suicide.

It is not unheard of for a teacher who would not hesitate to get help for a friend to believe that a student who is talking about suicide is not serious, or can be talked out of the planned action, or is not capable of carrying out a threatened suicide. As child and adolescent psychologists report, young people do not think through the long-term ramifications of a suicide attempt. There is also, among some young people, a fascination with death as can be seen by the idolization of famous people who have died young or committed suicide.

If a student tells a teacher that he or she is going to harm self or others, the teacher must reveal that information even if a promise of confidentiality has been given. In a number of lawsuits brought against teachers and school districts, parents sought damages from teachers who were told by students in confidence that they planned to harm themselves or others; the teachers did not contact parents or other authorities. In some cases, the educators were held to be negligent by failing to warn.

Legal immunity

As reviewed in Chapter Four, it is a widely held myth that counselors, physicians, psychologists, and social workers have legal immunity from responsibility for any injuries that may arise from their not acting on confidential information presented to them. Most states have abolished counselor immunity, and the few who still "have it on the books" have imposed several limitations on the concept. A counselor who hears from a young person that the individual plans to kill his or her parents and does nothing about it will not be legally able to decline to answer questions under oath nor will the counselor be held harmless for any resulting injuries if he or she decides not to revel the threats. Counselors and teachers must make it very clear to confiding individuals that they will keep their confidences unless health, life or safety or those of another are involved.

The only two privileges from disclosure of confidentiality information which seem to remain in state law are that of priest/penitent and attorney/client. Even the husband/wife privilege which allowed a spouse to refuse to testify against a spouse has been largely abandoned.

In light of the above facts, a teacher must presume that no legal protection exists for those who receive student confidences. What should the teacher who wants to be a role model for young persons, who wants to be approachable and helpful do? The answer is simple: lay down the ground rules for confidentiality before you receive any confidences. Tell students you will respect their confidences except in cases of life, health and safety. If a student asks to talk to you in confidence, reiterate the ground rules before the students begins to share.

Journal writing

Religion, language arts, English and other subject matter teachers have long recognized the value of student journal writing. This practice does, however, carry a real risk of student disclosure of information that the teacher is compelled to reveal. Teachers must set the same rules for confidentiality as are discussed above.

Teachers must understand that they *are* expected to read what students write. If a teacher cannot read the assignment, then the assignment should not be made. In particular, teachers should avoid such techniques as telling students to clip together pages they do not wish the teacher to read or to write at the top of such pages, "Please do not read." Journal writing has a place in today's curriculum, but teachers must be sure that students understand the parameters of the assignment and of the teacher's responsibilities for reporting threatened danger.

Retreats

The retreat experience is extremely important for today's Catholic young people. However, students are often at their most vulnerable in such situations. They may share stories of child abuse, sexual harassment, family dysfunction, even possible criminal activity. While encouraging students to share, the group leader must once again set the ground rules before the sharing beings. The use of peer leaders does not lessen the responsibility of the supervising adults. Students leaders must be told of the ground rules and of the necessity to communicate them to group members as well as procedures to be followed in notifying adults if matter is revealed in sessions that must be reported.

Case law

In one case, *Brooks v. Logan and Joint District No. 2*, (1995), parents of a student who had committed suicide filed an action for wrongful death and a claim for negligent infliction of emotional distress against a teacher who had assigned the keeping of journals to her class. Jeff Brooks was a student at Meridian High School and was assigned to Ms. Logan's English class. Students were asked to make entries into a daily journal as part of their English composition work. For a period of four months prior to his death, Jeff wrote in his journal.

After his death, Ms. Logan read through the entries and gave the journal to a school counselor, who delivered it to Jeff's parents. Jeff had made journal entries which indicated that he was depressed and that he was contemplating suicide. One entry read as follows:

> Well, Edgar Allen Poe, I can live with studying about that stuff he wrote especially the one short story about the evil eye. . . . I used to write poems until I pronounced myself dead in one of them and how could I write poems or stories if I was dead. . . .
>
> Recently . . . see I went into a medium depression and wrote poems to two special people. . . . I told them it was too bad that I had to say goodbye this way like that but, it would be the only way and I felt better. . . . (p. 81)

Ms. Logan maintained that Jeff had requested that she not read his entries, so that he would feel free to express himself. The journal contained a note in which Ms. Logan stated that she would not read the journal for content, but would only check for dates and length. The parents maintained that, in a conversation with Ms. Logan after their receipt of the journal, she stated that she had "reread the entries." Ms. Logan denied that she made that statement, and contends that she did not read the entries in question until after Jeff's death.

The lower court granted summary judgment in favor of the teacher and the school district. However, the appellate court reversed the finding, and held that there were issues of fact in existence which could only be determined at trial.

Thus, a trial court will have to determine whether Ms. Logan's actions or inactions constituted negligence contributing to Jeff's death. Part of the analysis will have to include a determination as to whether Jeff's suicide was foreseeable: would a reasonable person in Ms. Logan's place have recognized the possibility of suicide and notified someone? The appellate court refers to similar case law in which jailers have been held liable for the suicide of prisoners when the prisoners had exhibited warning signs.

Conclusion

This case and the discussion indicate the vulnerability of teachers who receive student confidences. The wise Catholic educator will establish and enforce ground rules for dealing with student confidences, and will seek help from school officials and/or parents when appropriate.

For Reflection and Discussion

- Do your students know what your rules are concerning keeping student confidences? If your principal asks you to explain those rules, how would you respond?

- Student D asks to see you after school. She says that her friend, Student E, is pregnant and planning to terminate her pregnancy. E has not told her parents but D & E both think E's parents will force her to have an abortion, even if she objects. What will you do?

CHAPTER SIX

CHILD ABUSE AND NEGLECT

Statutory considerations

Defining abuse

In-service education

Who should file the report?

Teachers and abuse

For Reflection and Discussion

CHAPTER SIX

CHILD ABUSE AND NEGLECT

O ne of the most serious issues confronting educators today is child abuse. The media carry daily reports of adults causing children physical and emotional pain. The educator is in a particularly sensitive position. Adolescents often choose teachers as confidantes in their struggles to deal with abuse and its effects. For this reason, principals must ensure that teachers and all school employees are as prepared as possible to deal with the realities of abuse and neglect. Principals would be well advised to spend some time reviewing pertinent state law and school policies and providing at least a few minutes of discussion on the topic at one of the first faculty meetings of the year. If a separate meeting is not provided for other school employees such as secretaries, custodians and cafeteria workers, the principal should consider having them present for the appropriate portion of the faculty meeting.

Statutory considerations

All fifty states have laws requiring educators to report suspected abuse and/or neglect. While the actual wording varies from state to state, the statute will ordinarily be somewhat like that in Kentucky Revised Statutes 199.335(2):

> Any physician, osteopathic physician, nurse, teacher, school personnel, social worker…child-caring personnel…who knows or has reasonable cause to believe that a child is an abused or neglected child, shall report or cause a report to be made in accordance

with the provisions of this section. When any of the above persons is attending a child as part of his professional duties, he shall report or cause a report to be made.

Statutes generally mandate reporting procedures. The reporting individual usually makes a phone report which is followed by a written report within a specified time period, often 48 hours, although some states do have different procedures.

Statutes usually provide protection for a person who makes a good-faith report of child abuse which later is discovered to be unfounded. Such a good-faith reporter will not be liable to the alleged abuser for defamation of character. However, a person can be held liable for making what is referred to as a "malicious report," one which has no basis in fact and which was made by a person who knows that no factual basis existed. Conversely, statutes usually mandate that a person who knew of child abuse or neglect and failed to report it can be fined and/or charged with a misdemeanor or felony.

Defining abuse

What is child abuse? This author once heard an attorney define it as "corporal punishment gone too far." Although it excludes sexual abuse, the definition has merit. However, it poses questions: How far is too far? Who makes the final determination? Can what one person considers abuse be considered valid parental corporal punishment by another? Are there any allowances for differing cultural practices? It is difficult, if not impossible, to give a precise definition that will cover all eventualities. Certainly, some situations are so extreme that there can be little argument that abuse has occurred. A student who appears at school with cigarette burns has been abused by someone. When a child alleges sexual abuse, there probably exist only two conclusions: either the child is telling the truth or the child is lying. The investigating agency will have to determine which conclusion is true.

The majority of cases will probably not be clear-cut and an educator may well struggle to decide if a report should be made. Many law enforcement officials and some attorneys instruct educators to report everything that students tell them that could possibly constitute abuse or negligence. They further caution teachers that it is not their job to determine if abuse has occurred. As a reporter, the teacher's function is to present the information. Appropriate officials will determine whether the report should be investigated further or simply "screened out" as a well-intentioned report that does not appear to be in the category of abuse.

In-service education

School administrators should provide teachers, other employees and volunteers with some in-service training concerning the indicators of child abuse and neglect, and the legal procedures for reporting such conditions. There are many excellent written resources available. Local police departments and social service agencies are usually happy to make both materials and speakers available to schools. If a school does not provide its teachers with education and materials on this topic, a phone call to appropriate sources should provide the teacher with needed materials.

Some of the most helpful material will identify warning signs or situations that should alert persons that abuse my be happening. For example, the National Center for Child Abuse and Neglect Specialized Training has identified the following six indicators of child neglect:

(1) lack of supervision,
(2) lack of adequate clothing and good hygiene,
(3) lack of medical or dental care,
(4) lack of adequate education,
(5) lack of adequate nutrition, and
(6) lack of adequate shelter.

The center cautions persons to be sensitive to issues of poverty versus neglect. Poverty is not synonymous with neglect. Poor children may need social services; they may or may not be neglected or abused.

The National Center states that children who are abused physically or emotionally will display certain types of behavior which are survival responses to what is occurring in the home. Four categories of these behaviors include:

(1) overly compliant, passive, undemanding behaviors;
(2) extremely aggressive, demanding, and rageful behaviors;
(3) role-reversed "parental" behavior or extremely dependent behavior; and
(4) lags in development.

Who should file the report?

Many experts advise that the school administrator, usually the principal, make all child abuse and/or neglect reports, so that the same person is reporting all situations in a given school. However, individual state laws vary on this point. Each staff member must understand that, if for some reason the principal refuses to make the report, the staff member must file the report. If a staff member files a report, the principal should be notified that a report has been made. It is legally dangerous for the school when a police officer or other official appears to investigate a report of child abuse, and the principal does not know that a report has been filed.

Schools officials should decide in advance how visits and requests from police or social workers will be handled. Many states require that school personnel allow officials to examine and question students. Principals should seek legal counsel in determining the applicable law for a given state. If the law permits the examination and questioning of a child, a school official should always ask to be present. In some jurisdictions, the investigating official may refuse to allow school personnel to be present.

Teachers and abuse

A survey of educational cases decided in courts of record reveals that the number of lawsuits alleging teacher or other school employee abuse of children is increasing. While administrators can be found responsible for the acts of subordinates, courts appear unwilling to hold administrators liable unless there is clear evidence of administrative misconduct. In the 1990 case, *Medlin v. Bass*, school officials were found innocent of misconduct in their supervision of an educator guilty of abuse. The abuser's crime was outside the scope of employment and there were no compelling reasons for his superiors to investigate his background more thoroughly than they did. In the 1990 case, *D.T. et al. v. Ind. School District No. 16 of Pawnee County*, the court declined to hold school officials responsible for teacher abuse of students occurring during summer fund raising; a particularly troubling aspect of this case was the fact that the teacher had a previous conviction for sodomy. The decision notwithstanding, it is possible that, in situations in which a school employee has a criminal record involving child abuse, other courts may find administrators guilty of negligence if they failed to take reasonable steps to check references.

It is well established that schools can attract persons with abusive tendencies who are seeking children upon whom to prey. Thus, it is important that school officials do everything in their power to investigate the background of persons before employment.

Some states now mandate that persons who work with children be fingerprinted; each applicant must also sign an authorization of a police check of his or her name for any criminal arrests and/ or convictions. Conviction of a crime is not an automatic, permanent bar to employment. Many states bar persons who have been convicted of a violent crime in ten years immediately preceding employment. On employment applications, administrators may wish to include a statement such as: "Conviction of a crime is not an automatic bar to employment. Please provide all pertinent details. Decisions will be made as required by law."

Any student or parent complaint alleging child abuse by a teacher must be taken seriously. Failure to do so can put the school and its officials at grave legal risk. Administrators and school boards should adopt policies governing reporting child abuse/neglect by staff *before* the need for such policies surfaces. It is preferable to have a policy that is never needed then to have no policy and be forced to try to construct one when faced with a need.

For Reflection and Discussion

- If asked, how would you define child abuse?

- Student Z, whom you taught last year, asked to see you. She tells you that she has been tied to a chair in a dark, unheated closet and her father pours water from a pitcher on her head. She is left there in freezing weather. She asks you to turn her father in to the authorities so that he will get off her back. What will you do?

CHAPTER SEVEN

SEXUAL HARASSMENT: WHAT IS IT? WHAT DOES IT MEAN FOR THE CATHOLIC SCHOOL TEACHER?

Actions that can be "harassment"

Suggested policies

Prevention

For Reflection and Discussion

CHAPTER SEVEN

SEXUAL HARASSMENT: WHAT IS IT? WHAT DOES IT MEAN FOR THE CATHOLIC SCHOOL TEACHER?

Today's Catholic educator has probably heard much about sexual harassment. Newspapers carry stories of alleged sexual harassment and resulting law suits. No longer is sexual harassment something that is found only between two adults or between an adult and a child. School children claim that they have been harassed by peers. The news stories can seem overwhelming, and the potential for legal liability great. What, then, can the Catholic school teacher do?

Administrators and teachers should first ensure that they understand what sexual harassment is. Every comment that is made concerning gender is not sexual harassment. For example, a male student who states, "Everyone knows boys are better at math than girls," or a teacher who declares, "I'd rather teach girls since they are not as rowdy as boys," is not guilty of sexual harassment, but may be guilty of a new tort recognized in some states as gender harassment. Title VII of the Civil Rights Act of 1964 mandated that the workplace be free of harassment based on sex. Title IX requires that educational programs receiving federal funding be free of sexual harassment. Both these titled laws are anti-discrimination statutes.

Federal anti-discrimination law can bind Catholic institutions. Most schools now file statements of compliance with discrimination laws with appropriate local, state and national authorities. Anti-discrimination legislation can impact Catholic schools because the government has a compelling interest in the equal treatment of all citizens. Compliance with statutory law can be required if there is no less burdensome way to meet the requirements of the law. Regardless of the applicability of the law, fairness requires that schools strive to be fair in the administration of all programs.

The Equal Employment Opportunities Commission has issued guidelines which define sexual harassment, forbidden by Title VII as: Unwelcomed sexual advances, requests for sexual favors, and other verbal or physical conduct of a sexual nature when:

- Submission to such conduct by an individual is made explicitly or implicitly a term of employment;
- Submission to, or rejection of such conduct by an individual is used as the basis for an employment decision and;
- Such conduct has the purpose or effect to interfere with an individual's work performance, or creates a hostile or intimidating environment.

Courts, including the U.S. Supreme Court, are vigorously supporting persons' rights to be free from sexual harassment.

In the 1992 case of *Franklin v. Gwinnet County Public Sch..*, the United States Supreme Court ruled that monetary damages can be awarded students whose rights under Title IX have been violated. In this case a teacher had allegedly sexually harassed a student for several years. The harassment consisted of conversations, kissing, telephone calls and forced sexual relations. The school system maintained that no relief could be given the student since Title IX remedies had been limited to back pay and employment relief. The court disagreed, held that students who suffer harassment are entitled to damages, and remanded the case to the lower court for a determination of damages. Thus, it would appear that if Title IX applies to the Catholic school, students are protected against sexual harassment in much the same manner that employees are protected.

Actions that can be "harassment"

The following are examples of behaviors that could constitute sexual harassment: sexual propositions, off-color jokes, inappropriate physical contact, innuendos, sexual offers, looks, and gestures. In a number of recent public school cases, female students alleged that male students made sexual statements to them and that school officials, after being informed, declined to take action and stated that "boys will be boys." Many of these cases have been settled out of court and money has been paid to the alleged victims.

Although one can argue that the person who sexually harasses another should be liable and not the school and its administrators, case law is suggesting that administrators who ignore such behavior or do not take it seriously can be held liable to the offended parties. (See the 1990 case, *Jane Doe v. Special Sch. Dist. of St. Louis County.*)

Suggested policies

One of the most important actions an administrator can take with regard to sexual harassment is to develop clear policies defining sexual harassment and detailing procedures for dealing with claims that sexual harassment has occurred. Teachers and other staff members are required to implement the policies. The following is one suggestion of a policy statement:

Sexual harassment is defined as:

(1) threatening to impose adverse employment, academic or disciplinary or other sanctions on a person, unless favors are given; and/or

(2) conduct, containing sexual matter or suggestions, which would be offensive to a reasonable person.

Sexual harassment includes, but is not limited to, the following behaviors:

(1) Verbal conduct such as epithets, derogatory jokes or comments, slurs or unwanted sexual advances, imitations, or comments;

(2) Visual contact such as derogatory and/or sexually oriented posters, photography, cartoons, drawings, or gestures;

(3) Physical contact such as assault, unwanted touching, blocking normal movements, or interfering with work, study, or play because of sex;

(4) Threats and demands to submit to sexual requests as a condition of continued employment or grades or other benefits or to avoid some other loss and offers of benefits in return for sexual favors; and

(5) Retaliation for having reported or threatened to report sexual harassment.

Procedures for reporting should then be given. These procedures should include a statement such as, "All allegations will be taken seriously and promptly investigated." Confidentiality should be stressed. Concern should be expressed for both the alleged victim and the alleged perpetrator. Any forms that are to be used should be included in the procedures.

Every employee should be required to sign a statement that he or she has been given a copy of the policies relating to sexual harassment and other sexual misconduct, has read the material, and agrees to be bound by it. Parent/student handbooks should contain at least a general statement that sexual harassment is not condoned in a Christian atmosphere, and both parents and students should sign a statement that they agree to be governed by the handbook.

Prevention

It is far easier to prevent claims of sexual harassment than it is to defend them. To that end, teachers and other employees should participate in appropriate in-service training that raises awareness of sexual harassment and other gender issues. Staff members must understand what sorts of behaviors can be construed as sexual harassment.

Teachers should discuss issues of fair treatment of others with their students, and should promptly correct any students who demean others. Defenses such as, "I was only kidding," will not be accepted if the alleged victim states that the behavior was offensive and unwelcome, and a court finds that a reasonable person could find the behavior offensive and unwelcome.

Finally, of course, sexual harassment and other forms of demeaning behavior have no place in a Catholic school. Guarding the dignity of each member of the school community should be a priority for all Catholic educators.

For Reflection and Discussion

- Can you define sexual harassment if asked to do so by a parent or student?

- How would you handle the following scenario? You are supervising a student mixer. You see a thirteen year old girl sitting by the bathroom and weeping. You ask what is wrong. She gives you the name of a male student and says, "He told me my cup size has to be bigger than my head. I'm afraid to go back on the dance floor. Am I really so big?"

CHAPTER EIGHT

STUDENTS WITH SPECIAL NEEDS IN CATHOLIC SCHOOLS: WHAT IS THE CATHOLIC EDUCATOR'S RESPONSIBILITY?

Discrimination law

Public Law 94-142

Standards of supervision discipline

The Americans with Disabilities Act: What does it require?

The right to the best education

A concluding thought

Case law

For Reflection and Discussion

CHAPTER EIGHT

STUDENTS WITH SPECIAL NEEDS IN CATHOLIC SCHOOLS: WHAT IS THE CATHOLIC EDUCATOR'S RESPONSIBILITY?

Today's Catholic school teachers face many challenges, including the possibility of litigation against Catholic schools brought by parents of students with special needs who are seeking admission and/or retention.

Section 504 of the Rehabilitation Act of 1973 and the 1992 ADA can seem like a legal quagmire for the educator. Myths and half-truths abound. Some consultants and lawyers advise that schools must be made totally accessible. Many administrators fear that the cost of accommodations will be so high as to force schools out of existence. Other administrators question the appropriateness of accepting students with special needs in college prep schools. Can the average Catholic school provide the proper program adjustments needed by these students? Catholic school personnel need a clear understanding of legal requirements.

Discrimination law

Federal law prohibits discrimination on the basis of race, sex, disability, age and national origin. Although discrimination on the basis of religion or creed is also prohibited, the right of reli-

gious institutions to give preference to their own members is up-
held. Practically, this means that Catholic schools may give preference to Catholic students and may give hiring preference to
Catholic teachers and other employees.

Public Law 94-142

Catholic school administrators must understand the law governing students with special needs. Public Law 94-142, The Education of All Handicapped Children Act, ensures a "free and appropriate education" for all children. There is no requirement that
Catholic schools provide the "free and appropriate education."
However, in situations in which the only school for the handi-
capped/disabled is one operated by the Catholic Church or some
other private organization, the state may place a child in a private
school if that placement seems to provide the most appropriate
education. In such a case, the state would be responsible for the
tuition.

Catholic schools are not required to meet every need of every
child. Most private schools are not equipped to offer educational
services to everyone. The fact that a school does not have to offer
services does not mean that a student attending that school has
no right to such services. Public Law 94-142 and IDEA gives students rights; a private school student has a right to request and
receive an evaluation and, if necessary, an individual educational
plan (IEP). The public school must make every reasonable effort
to provide the student with services needed even if the student
remains in the private school. If it is not practical to offer such
services to a private school student, the public school officials can
draw up an IEP which calls for public school education. A parent
is always free to accept or reject such an IEP. If a parent elects to
keep a child in a private school over the objections of the professional educators working with that child, the public school cannot
be held responsible for the child's progress nor can the public
school be required to pay private school tuition.

It is important to note that the private school student and the
public school student have the same federal protections. The private school student is entitled to the same services a public school
student is entitled to receive; however, the private school student
may not be able to insist that the services be provided within a
private school as part of an IEP.

Both the *Zobrest v. Catalina Foothills School District* and *Agostini v.
Felton* demonstrate this reality. In *Zobrest*, the U.S. Supreme Court
ruled that the constitution did not prohibit the placing of a public
school employee as a sign language interpreter in a religious school.
The case has a narrow applicability, and public school districts

may take the position they are not bound by it; in such a case, a parent or private school seeking such an interpreter or other instructional aid would have to enter litigation to determine the applicability of *Zobrest* to the particular school or situation.

Standards of supervision

Principals, many of whom are familiar with the adage, "the younger the child chronologically or mentally, the greater the standard of care," may well ask, "If we accept students with special needs, are we committing ourselves to higher levels of supervision?"

Teachers can be held to different standards. For example, a teacher who is supervising a senior honors class will probably be held to a lower standard that would an individual teaching kindergarten children. Courts assume that older children can be expected to take some responsibility for themselves.

Mental age is concerned with the effect that a disability may have on a child. If a Catholic school accepts a student with a mental disability, teachers must accommodate the disability. If a child performs well below grade level and exhibits immature behavior, a teacher may be expected to provide more stringent supervision than that given to other students. Some disabilities are not mental, of course. If a child is an amputee, the child will need more supervision and help in physical activities than others may need.

Discipline

All students need to be accountable to persons in authority. Special needs children are no exception. Schools have the right to require that all students abide by codes of conduct. Every student in a Catholic school should be expected to obey the rules.

Exceptions are in order only when the infraction is the result of the disability. If students who use walkers or crutches cannot get to class on time because they simply cannot move fast enough, it would be unfair to penalize them for being late. Another example is presented by a student with Tourette's syndrome, which is often characterized by bizarre behavior such as swearing. If a student suffering from Tourette's were to use profanity, it might be unfair to discipline the student if the behavior is beyond the student's control.

The Americans with Disabilities Act: What does it require?

The Americans with Disabilities Act, like Section 504 of the Rehabilitation Act of 1973, requires that disabled persons be offered reasonable accommodations, those which an institution could be expected to fund. It would not be reasonable to suppose that a Catholic school should institute a special program, with special teachers, for a blind student or a profoundly mentally handicapped student.

Neither Section 504 of the Rehabilitation Act of 1974 nor the Americans with Disabilities Act requires that institutions create programs to meet the needs of the disabled. What these laws require is that institutions not discriminate against persons who are seeking admission to their programs. If a disabled person can participate in the program with a reasonable amount of accommodation, then the institution must provide the accommodation. If providing that support system would create a significant hardship, the institution will not have to provide it. For example, if a blind student were to seek admission and acceptance of that student would require that a special teacher be employed for the student and that all teachers learn Braille, the school would probably not be expected to incur those expenses.

Another significant issue, accessibility to facilities by all members of the public with a ligitimate right to be present at the school, must be addressed. Disabled parents have a moral and ethical right, as well as a possible legal right, to attend functions in which their children participate and to attend parent events, such as parent/teacher conferences. Although the applicability of the Americans with Disabilities Act to church- related institutions is being challenged, Gospel imperatives, as well as the doctrine of fairness, require that educators make every *reasonable* effort to accommodate. Reasonable effort does not usually mean spending hundreds of thousands of dollars to install elevators, but it may mean moving the parent / teacher conferences to a more accessible location, such as a gym.

It must be frankly stated, however, that simply because one is not legally required to do something, it does not follow that one should not do that thing, if it is the right thing to do. If a school has significant assets and could afford a sign language interpreter for a deaf student or instructions in signing for the faculty and staff, the educator may have a moral and ethical duty to provide for the student even though the law does not require such provision. Indeed, the Pastoral Statement of U.S. Catholic Bishops on Handicapped People (1978) seems to demand such action: "If handicapped people are to become equal partners in the Christian community, injustices must be eliminated." Certainly, Catholic schools should be leaders in fighting injustice wherever it is found, especially as it affects those whose disabilities place them among those for whom Christ manifested special concern.

The right to the best education

All students have the right to a "free and appropriate education," according to Public Law 94-142, the Education of All Handicapped Children Act. Students must be evaluated for special services at parental request, but the law does not entitle students to a special needs program. Catholic school students have the same right to evaluation as do public school students. However, the program recommended as a result of the evaluation may not be available in the Catholic school, which is only required to make reasonable accommodations.

Public Law 94-142 requires that students receive a "free and appropriate" education, but it does not require that the education be the best available. To require the best education would mean that school systems would constantly be meeting parental demands for instructional services that could "better" student performance.

As a result of the *Agostini* case which overturned the 1985 *Aguilar* decision, public schools can now provide services in religious schools. The key word is *can*. Can is not synonymous with must. Thus, public schools could still refuse to provide services in the Catholic school, so long as the students had access to them in the public school.

A concluding thought

Much apprehension could be alleviated if administrators clearly understood what the law does and does not require. In the final analysis, though, the question is not, "Did you do what you had to do?" but "Did you do what you could?"

Case law

In one case under the Individuals with Disabilities Education Act, the United States District Court for the Southern District of Texas held that the parents of a hearing impaired student were not entitled to reimbursement from the public school district for their unilateral change of their child to a private program. The parents disagreed with the particular program that the Individual Education Plan offered the student. The parents argued that since they did not believe that the public school program offered their child the best possible education, they should be allowed to enroll their child in the school they believed provided the best program; further, the parents claimed that the public school district was legally bound to reimburse them for the cost of the private school tuition. However, the student was making progress in an appropriate manner in the public school program in which she had been enrolled; thus, the court found that no reimbursement was in order. (See *Bonnie Ann F. by John. R. v. Calallen Independent School Dist.*)

In a similar case, *Doe by and Through Doe v. Board of Education of Tullahoma City Schools,* a federal appeals court held that a student's IEP met the standards of the Individuals with Disabilities Education Act. The student suffered from a neurological impairment which hindered his ability to process auditory information and use normal language and thinking skills; the IEP offered mainstreaming, with a provision for oral, rather than written examinations, and tutorial assistance. Although the parents contested the IEP, the court found that an appropriate education was being provided. Thus, the court declined to require the school board to reimburse parents for private tuition when they removed the student to a private program.

Both cases indicated that courts are reluctant to require reimbursement for private school tuition, if the program developed for a special needs student seems to provide an "appropriate" public education. Catholic school administrators should be wary of any parent of a special needs student who claims that tuition will be paid by a public school district.

For Reflection and Discussion

- A student with diagnosed learning disorders tells you that he will be taping your classes from now on "because the doctor said it would help." How do you respond?

- The principal has brought a "problem" case to the faculty for advice. Mrs. K, who already has two children in your school and one who has graduated, has asked the school to admit her daughter who is totally blind. She says it will be no problem for the school to have materials translated into Braille and that student helpers can be assigned to her daughter to assist her in getting around he building. Do you think the school should accept this student? Why or why not? What legal issues do you see?

CHAPTER NINE

EXTRA-CURRICULAR AND CO-CURRICULAR ACTIVITIES: LEGAL ISSUES

Assignment and training of moderators

Student selection and standards for participation

Administrative monitoring

For Reflection and Discussion

CHAPTER NINE

EXTRA-CURRICULAR AND CO-CURRICULAR ACTIVITIES: LEGAL ISSUES

Extra-curricular and co-curricular activities have long been a part of secondary education. Such activities include, but are not limited to speech and debate clubs, athletic games/intramurals, and choir recitals, to name a few activities. With these activities comes an increased concern for legal issues.

It is not unusual for a busy administrator or activity sponsor to notice some problems with an activity and to promise oneself that next year will be different. Teachers who sponsor extra-curricular activities will understand their various responsibilities and will conscientiously perform their duties. Academic and behavioral requirements for extra-curricular participation will be published to all affected and enforced. Some plan for dealing with students who are dropped off for practices or activities well before an adult supervisor is present or who are still present on campus long after activities will be in place. However, as any seasoned educator knows, next years come all too soon.

Faculty and staff should be involved in the development of a plan for improvement of the programs offered. Staff members should be encouraged to submit their suggestions for improvement in writing. Thus, as the season closes, the administrator and moderator can meet to determine policies and procedures for the coming year.

Extra-curricular and co-curricular activities are, by their very nature, more dangerous than ordinary classroom activities. Participants and their parents can appear to care far more passionately about extra-curricular programs than about curriculum offerings. An angry student or parent can always threaten a lawsuit. The reasonable educator will not be unduly alarmed when threats are made; if policies and procedures are properly developed and implemented, the administrator will be in the best possible position.

Assignment and training of moderators

The assignment of moderators at the beginning of the year and the replacement of moderators during the year can present critical challenges for the administrator. There is a great temptation to take anyone who expresses interest in the activity and make that person the moderator. Such a procedure is particularly dangerous in athletics, which will be discussed in greater detail in the next chapter. While a person does not need to be an expert wrestler to coach wrestling or an outstanding actor to direct the play, the individual should be willing to study the requirements for coaching a team or directing a play. At the same time, persons who played a sport or acted in a play may believe that they can direct the activity when, in fact, participation does not ensure the ability to teach another the skill. Administrators must ensure that persons who moderate activities possess at least minimum understanding of the activity. For example, released time, or other incentives, can be provided to allow a neophyte moderator to visit a more experienced one or to choose a mentor at another school. Such actions may be time-consuming, but they provide the best protection for the safety of students and the best defense against liability in the case of injury.

The applicant's experience and qualifications to serve as a moderator must be verified. If one has no actual experience participating in the activity, one should be able to indicate how one has or will acquire the necessary knowledge or skills. If the moderator appears to be truly inexperienced and untried, that individual should not be assigned complete responsibility for the students participating the activity, but could be assigned as an assistant to a more experienced faculty member.

Secondary school educators may ask whether using a volunteer as a moderator is very advisable. There are certainly times and occasions when such an action may be best. If someone's mother had extensive experience in college musicals, she may be able to direct the school play; she may even be more qualified to do so than anyone on the faculty. A student's father who was a football captain may be able to serve as an outstanding coach. While the use of volunteers is certainly legally acceptable, the principal or other administrator must ensure that the individual is a person of integrity and trustworthiness. Some states require fingerprinting before individuals are allowed to work with young persons on a regular basis. At the very least, the administrator should ask for references and check them, so that persons with pedophile tendencies and charming personalities are not inadvertently assigned to positions of great trust. While no one can avert every possible tragedy, the wise administrator will have some procedure in place to gather the necessary background information concerning volunteers.

Diocesan and/or local administrators should consider an annual orientation for extracurricular moderators. Athletic coaches may be offered a separate orientation. In the unfortunate event of an injury, educational administrators could demonstrate that they had taken their responsibilities seriously and had tried to ensure that moderators and coaches were competent.

Student selection and standards for participation

Most administrators have been the recipients of parent and/or student complaints regarding non-selection for an activity. Administrators should insist that moderators and coaches develop, publish, and implement clear standards for selection. Obviously, selection is a subjective process. Feelings do get hurt. The administrator who insists on clear standards and monitors the performance of moderators and coaches can be satisfied that the requirements of fairness are met. The administrator should guard against taking the side of a parent or student in a dispute over selection for, or retention in, an activity unless the moderator/coach is clearly in the wrong. One of the worst situations for a moderator and administrator to be in is one in which the administrator "second guesses" the decisions of the moderator.

Each activity and each moderator will have some rules and regulations to which the student participant must adhere. Some may be general school rules. Others may be specific to the activity. Further, in the case of athletics and drama, for example, state associations may provide other standards.

Rules and regulations should be standardized as far as possible. It seems very unfair for an athlete with a failing grade to be "benched," while another student with a similar grade is allowed to sing the lead in the school play. Everyone who participates in extra-curricular activities should abide by some common code of conduct.

Some rules and regulations that might be considered could include:

- attendance during the school day in order to participate in an activity;
- academic requirements (minimum grade averages, for example) for participation;
- behavior requirements (a student who is suspended from school should not be participating in an extra-curricular activity).

Administrative monitoring

School administrators need to be familiar with the rules and regulations of every activity in their schools. Certainly, they cannot be expected to recall every rule at any given moment; but, they should have access to every rule and be able to obtain it if they cannot summon it from memory.

Key administrators need to be physically present at athletic events and other extra-curricular activities. No principal should be expected to be at every game or activity, but chief administrators should ensure that there is some administrative supervision throughout the course of the year. Regular meetings with moderators and coaches can also keep everyone informed and help to minimize problems.

For Reflection and Discussion

- Your principal has asked you to become the moderator of the fencing club. You have never fenced in your life. Your principal states that all you have to do is be present at practices and games; he/she insists that you don't need to know anything about fencing. How will you respond?

- The parents of Student Q have just come to your classroom without an appointment. Q did not get a major role in the school play you direct. The parents state that last year's director (who has moved to another school) promised that Q would get a big part if Q took acting lessons from him at the rate of $50 an hour. The parents want Q to have a major part, or in the alternative, a refund of the $2,000 spent on acting lessons. What will you say and/or do?

CHAPTER TEN

ATHLETICS: SOME LEGAL CONCERNS

Avoiding negligence

The duty to supervise

Violation of duty

Proximate cause

Injury

Grading and exclusion from athletics

Conclusion

For Reflection and Discussion

CHAPTER TEN

ATHLETICS: SOME LEGAL CONCERNS

Athletics, like all extra-curricular activities, pose some of the greatest legal concerns for secondary schools, and programs in Catholic schools are no exception. Principals, athletic directors, and teachers constantly ask themselves how they can best protect student athletes from injury and the school from liability.

Avoiding negligence

Most lawsuits alleging negligence begin in the classroom, since that is where students spend most of their time. Other areas, however, are potentially more dangerous than the classroom, hence, a greater standard of care will be expected from staff and administrators. School athletic programs are clearly activities that are more dangerous than normal classroom activities.

Negligence is an unintentional act or omission which results in injury. Persons who bring successful negligence suits are usually awarded financial damages in an amount calculated to compensate for the actual injury suffered. Punitive or exemplary damages can also be awarded. In assessing whether a person's behavior is negligent, a court will use the "reasonable person" test: would a reasonable person in the defendant's situation have acted in this manner? "Reasonable" is whatever the jury or other fact-finder decided it is.

Before a court will find a defendant legally negligent, four elements, previously discussed in Chapter Two, must be present: *duty, violation of duty, proximate cause,* and *injury.* An examination of each of the four elements as applied to athletics should prove helpful to persons supervising athletic programs.

The duty to supervise

The individual charged with negligence must have a *duty* in the situation. Student athletes have a right to safety and coaches and other officials have a responsibility to protect the well-being of all those entrusted to their care. Coaches are assumed to have a duty to provide reasonable supervision of their players. It is expected that principals and athletic directors will have developed and promulgated rules and regulations which guide coaches in providing for student safety. Coaches should develop and implement further team practices that are consistent with safety and in harmony with administrative practices.

Violation of duty

Negligence cannot exist if the second element, *violation of duty,* is not present. Courts understand that accidents and spontaneous actions can occur. The 1989 New York case, *Benitez v. NYC Board of Education,* involved a high school football player who was injured during play. The player alleged negligence on the part of the coach and principal for allowing him to play in a fatigued condition.

A lower court awarded the student damages, but the appellate court ruled that school officials had to provide only reasonable, not extraordinary, care and reversed the decision. Further, the court invoked the doctrine of *assumption of the risk.* Students are under no compulsion to play sports; if they choose to participate, they voluntarily assume the risks of some injuries. *Assumption of the risk* is a defense against an allegation of negligence.

At first glance, it may appear that athletic directors and coaches are the school officials who would be found liable for violation of duty in the case of student injury. Under the doctrine of *respondent superior,* let the superior answer, principals and administrators can be found liable for the acts of subordinates. For example, if a principal paid little or no attention to the administration of the athletic program, provided no supervision, and/or offered no guidance, he or she might well be found guilty of negligence if a student were to be injured, while a dangerous practice or policy was in place. Unfortunately, many administrators believe themselves to be woefully ignorant of the principles of athletics and are too often content to let coaches and athletic directors run the whole sports program unsupervised. These same administrators would be shocked if someone were to suggest that a second year English teacher is an expert, needs no supervision, and should be given *carte blanche* in directing his classes.

Principals have an obligation to oversee athletics, while teachers must support the regulation of the athletic program. Certainly no one expects a principal to be an athletic expert, but the principal should be sure that only qualified individuals are hired as coaches and athletic directors. The principal should insist that the athletic director and/or coaches keep the administrator and teachers informed about the operation of the program.

Every principal and athletic director should seriously consider having an athletic handbook outlining the policies and procedures for each sport. Parents and students should sign a statement agreeing to be governed by the provisions of the handbook.

Principals will not be held responsible for every mistake of employees but only for those which a reasonable person could have foreseen. In the 1979 Virginia case, *Short v. Griffits*, an athletic director was held liable for injuries sustained by a student who fell on broken glass while running laps. The school and the school board were exonerated. It was the athletic director's responsibility to ensure that the playing areas and equipment were in order. Unless the principal had some reason to believe that the employee was careless in supervision, the principal would not be expected to check the area for hazards.

Proximate cause

The third requirement for legal negligence is *proximate cause*. The violation of duty must be the proximate cause of the injury. Proximate cause is sometimes defined as contributing factor. If a coach were to order a 250-pound student to wrestle a 125-pound student and the lighter student were injured in the match, the coach is the proximate cause of the injury even though the physical actions of the heavier student are the direct cause of the injury.

The court must decide whether proper performance of duty could have prevented the injury and, in so doing, the court has to look at the facts of each individual case. In an old, but still applicable 1970 case, *Stehn v. MacFadden Foundations*, a private school and its officials were held liable for damages sustained by a student who suffered a severe spinal cord injury in a wrestling match. The court found that the maneuver which resulted in the injury was not listed in any reputable book on the subject of teaching wrestling, and the defense could produce no evidence that the maneuver was legitimate. The coach had very limited previous experience and was coaching without any supervision.

The court ruled that the school's violation of duty, its failure to ensure that the coach was qualified and experienced, was the proximate cause of the student's injury. Proximate cause is a complex doctrine. It is difficult to predict what a court will determine to be the proximate cause in any particular allegation of negligence.

Injury

The fourth element necessary for a finding of negligence is *injury*. To prevail in a lawsuit, a student must have sustained an injury for which the court can award a remedy. No matter how unreasonable the behavior of a coach, there is no legal negligence if there is no injury. Everyone must understand, however, that physical harm is not the only type of injury; emotional or psychological harm can also constitute injury.

Grading and exclusion from athletics

High school educators often face the problem of students who just barely miss attaining the necessary minimum grades to continue participation in a sport. Students, parents, and others can exert considerable pressure on teachers to change grades so that students can qualify to play. One might argue that such a practice is hardly the material of which lawsuits are made Even if no lawsuit is ever filed, there are issues of fairness.

One should note that problems result when minimum standards are lowered. If there is a rule requiring certain conduct or academic standards, educators should honor it. The rule should be adopted as school policy. Exceptions should be avoided.

Conclusion

Even if every possible precaution is taken, the possibility for student injury is very high. Educators have very real duties to ensure that only competent personnel-trained in coaching techniques, theory of the sport, and first aid/safety procedures-are employed. Further, policies should provide:

- clear procedures to be followed when accidents occur
- minimal delay in seeking medical attention when needed
- hazard-free equipment and playing areas.

There is no absolute protection against lawsuits, particularly in athletics. Nonetheless, a thorough handbook, as indicated earlier, can provide the best possible protection and can serve as evidence that both parents and students understand the risks involved in sports and the requirements of participation in the school athletic program.

For Reflection and Discussion

- If asked, how would you describe the role of athletics in your school? What legal and ethical responsibilities do teachers have?

- Student M, the star volleyball player, has asked you to give her one extra point on her grade so that she won't be suspended from the team and miss tournament play. She has offered to do extra work. Without M, there is very little chance that the team can win any of the tournament games. The coach has come to you on M's behalf, and you have a phone message that M's father, the chief justice of the state supreme court, has asked for a meeting with you. You must have a decision by 8:00A.M. tomorrow. What will you do?

CHAPTER ELEVEN

PERSONAL CONDUCT OF PROFESSIONAL STAFF: LEGAL ISSUES

Behavioral expectations for Catholic educators

Illegal activity

Relationships with students

Summary

For Reflection and Discussion

PERSONAL CONDUCT OF PROFESSIONAL STAFF: LEGAL ISSUES

A t some time or other, Catholic educational administrators confront the issues of actual or perceived inappropriate staff conduct, and may wonder what legal rights they have to demand certain standards of behavior from staff members, particularly during off-campus times. What a staff member does, both in and outside the educational setting, impacts the quality and integrity of ministry within the setting. The doctrine of separation of church and state protects administrators of religious institutions and allows them to set standards of personal behavior that would not be permitted in the public sector.

Behavioral expectations for Catholic educators

Catholic educational administrators should ensure that documents governing employment state that staff members are expected to support the teachings of the Catholic Church through their behavior. Obviously, many programs have non-Catholic staff members, and one would not expect such individuals to attend Mass outside the school on a regular basis or to be participating members of a parish. But, non-Catholics who seek to acquire or retain positions in Catholic settings should expect that standards of behavior will be in force. For example, if the fact that an individual has an abortion becomes known and is a source of scandal, the administrator has every right to terminate that individual's employment or volunteer status. To do otherwise may send a confusing message to parents, students, and the larger community.

Issues of sexual preference pose special problems. While no one should condemn a homosexual orientation, a Catholic educational administrator, as an agent of the Church, cannot ignore manifestations of a gay lifestyle that pose scandal.

Equally difficult decisions must be made in situations involving divorced teachers who remarry without an annulment and that fact becomes known. There is no easy solution but the administrator has an obligation to see that the teachings of the Catholic Church are respected and not compromised in the witness given by staff members. It should also be noted that many diocesan policies are concerned with public behavior that is a cause for scandal.

In summary, then, once an individual performs an act that is inconsistent with a teaching position in Church ministry, that person may no longer be qualified to minister in a given situation at a certain time. While such a reality may seem obvious, it is recommended that documents state the requirement of supporting the teachings of the Church.

Illegal activity

A person who has committed an illegal act may certainly have employment terminated. One who is convicted of, or who admits commission of, a crime should be removed from professional and/or volunteer status. The harder question arises when a person is simply accused of, or arrested on suspicion of, a crime. Educators may be sharply divided on the proper response to make in such a situation.

The United States has long operated under the principle of "innocent until proven guilty." It may appear that, until guilt is established, the fair approach would be to let the person continue in ministry. Yet, the reality is often that effectiveness in such situations is severely compromised.

How, then, should one deal with an arrest of, or serious accusation concerning, a staff member? Every educational entity should have a policy in place that allows the administrator to place the accused individual on a leave of absence pending the outcome of an investigation or an adjudication of guilt. The time to enact a policy is not when it is needed. The prudent administrator and educational board will have policy in place that anticipates such situations; it will be much easier to deal with an established policy and procedure when one is needed than to try to fashion a policy after the fact.

Relationships with students

Chapter Four offers discussion of the legal risks posed by student/staff relationships. Obviously, teachers want to demonstrate a personal interest in their students. It is a sad reality, however, that administrators must be vigilant in monitoring staff behavior in an effort to avoid even the appearance of impropriety.

Summary

While realizing the complexity inherent in many of the situations discussed above, the Catholic school must ensure that both fidelity to the Church and compliance with law characterize policies and procedures; the teacher must support the teachings of the Catholic Church.

For Reflection and Discussion

- You agreed to go on a blind date. You and your date "hit it off" and make plans to meet again. In the faculty room with several people present, someone asks you if you knew the person is a "fallen away" Catholic who has been married and divorced twice. How do you respond? What would you do?

- A student questions you in class one day, "Were you a virgin when you married?" or "Are you still a virgin?" How will you respond?

CHAPTER TWELVE

GANGS AND CATHOLIC EDUCATION: WHAT SHOULD ADMINISTRATORS AND STAFF DO?

Gang attire, symbols and behaviors

Disciplinary steps

Keeping a focus

For Reflection and Discussion

CHAPTER TWELVE

GANGS AND CATHOLIC EDUCATION: WHAT SHOULD ADMINISTRATORS AND STAFF DO?

In the last decade or so, the word "gang" has taken on a very different meaning than it had twenty, thirty, or fifty years ago. Many readers remember their parents or grand-parents referring to the good times they had while they "ran around with a gang of friends." Today, the word "gang" has taken on a sinister meaning connoting fear, violence, and domination. Sud-denly, it seems everyone is clamoring for schools to do something about the presence and activities of gangs. Many dioceses are writing and implementing policies concerning gangs.

The first step in developing policy is to define exactly what a gang is. A 1991 California case, *The People v. Ralph Gamez*, was significant in its definition of gangs. The court stated that the proper term to use when discussing problematic gangs is "crimi-nal gang-like behavior." Unless one's state law has a different term or definition, diocesan staff and/or local administrators would be well-advised to adopt such a designation.

An analysis of *Gamez* and similar cases leads to a clearer defini-tion of criminal gang-like activity. One archdiocese (Louisville,

Kentucky) offers this definition: "Criminal gang-like activity involving membership in a criminal gang is defined as an ongoing organization, association, or group of three or more persons, whether formal or informal, having as one of its primary activities the commission of one or more criminal acts." Thus, both educator and young person should understand that the intent to commit criminal acts is what distinguishes criminal gang-like activity from other types of group activities. Moreover, it is not membership in a gang in and of itself that is the problem; it is the criminal activity.

Some may be tempted to think that enumerating all possible criminal offenses is useful in policy writing. In actuality, the issue of gangs is one that is better dealt with in general, rather than specific, terms. The term, "criminal gang-like activity," includes all possible offenses; attempts to enumerate all offenses can result in omission of some, or an argument by an aggrieved student that what he or she did was not terroristic threatening or property damage, for example.

Gang attire, symbols and behaviors

The wearing of colors has long indicated membership in a gang. Any school is well within its rights to forbid such displays. However, it is not always easy to identify what exactly is the display of gang colors. In one state, for example, two university athletic teams have different school colors. So gang members wear university sweatshirts, jackets, etc. to denote their membership in a particular gang. Certainly, there is nothing wrong with wearing a college sweatshirt and it is very difficult, if not impossible, to determine who is supporting a team and who is displaying gang colors. Many public schools now require students to wear uniforms. While the constitutionality of this mandate has yet to be tested, one result is a lessening of the wearing of colors. Catholic educators should enforce uniform regulations and/or dress codes and be attentive to violations of the codes.

Disciplinary steps

If a teacher suspects or notices criminal gang-like activity at any time during educational and related activities, the principal or other chief administrator should be notified immediately.

Second, the administrator should seek appropriate advice concerning investigation of the suspicion or allegation, and should then proceed to gather necessary data. Third, if the administrator determines or strongly suspects that the young person is involved in criminal gang-like activity, the student's parents or guardians should be notified and disciplinary action taken when appropriate. In the case of suspicion without any convincing evidence, a warning concerning the consequences for anyone who engages in criminal gang-like activity may be given. Written documentation of any meetings should be kept.

Fourth, if a criminal act has occurred, the administrator has a legal responsibility to notify local law enforcement officials and to assist the officials as far as possible in their investigation(s).

Keeping a focus

An educator should focus on what was actually done that is/ was wrong, rather than on membership in a gang. If a school rule has been broken, the breaking of the rule should be discussed and appropriate sanctions given. If a crime has been committed, the focus should be on the crime and its consequences.

Sometimes, a student needs help to avoid or terminate membership in a gang. Counselors should have some training or know where to contact trained persons so that student can be helped in avoiding gangs.

The days of simply announcing that some activity or association is wrong and expecting immediate students compliance are gone. It is every educator's responsibility to help in the creation of a Christian community in which persons have no desire to engage in criminal gang-like activity.

For Reflection and Discussion

- If your school has a gang policy do you believe it is adequate? Why or why not? If your school does not have such a policy, do you think one should be developed or implemented? What do you think should be included in the policy?

- Student H has approached you after school. She tells you that she is "in deep" with a gang whose members are planning a series of house robberies over the weekend. H has seen the guns that gang intends to use. H wants out of the gang, but fears bodily harm if she leaves. She asks your advice. What do you say? do?

CHAPTER THIRTEEN

COPYRIGHT LAW, TECHNOLOGY, AND CYBERSPACE

Reasons to copy

Copyright law

What is fair use?

Guidelines

Technology: Moral, ethical, and legal challenges

Appropriateness of materials available

Conclusion

For Reflection and Discussion

CHAPTER THIRTEEN

COPYRIGHT LAW, TECHNOLOGY, AND CYBERSPACE

Most educators realize that copyright law exists. If asked, many would probably respond that there are rules that should be followed when making copies of articles, book chapters, computer programs and television programs. Teachers have seen notices warning persons making copies on copy machines that they are subject to the provisions of the copyright law.

For some individuals, the fact that apprehension and prosecution for breaking the copyright law rarely become reality becomes a license to break the law. For others, their motive of helping students to learn is an excuse for failing to comply with the law.

One commentator has observed: "Although this act [copying] may appear innocent on the surface, copyright infringement, whether malicious or not, is a criminal act. One's position as a teacher and having 'only the best interests of your students at heart' does not give anyone the right to copy indiscriminately." (Merickel, *The Educator's Rights to Fair Use of Copyrighted Work*).

Reasons to copy

In the 1960s and 1970s budgetary considerations were the reasons given by churches, including Catholic churches, that copied songs from copyrighted works and used the copies to compile parish hymnals. Courts have consistently struck down such uses and have ordered the offending churches to pay damages.

Today, churches appear to be aware of the legal consequences of copying and many subscribe to the licensing arrangements of music companies: for a given sum of money, the institution can make as many copies of music as desired during the span of the contract.

However, it is not uncommon to find teachers copying such items as whole workbooks, other consumable materials, large portions of books and print materials. The swift advance of technology has catapulted computer programs, videocassettes and similar media into the sphere of teacher copying.

This chapter will discuss copyright law as it applies to educational institutions, examine the tests of "fair use," and offer some guidelines for secondary school principals and teachers.

Copyright law

Upon reflection, most educators would agree that copyright protection is a just law. Both the Copyright Act of 1909 (the Old Law) and the Copyright Act of 1976 (the New Law) represent attempts to safeguard the rights of authors. Persons who create materials are entitled to the fruits of their labors; those who use author's creations without paying royalties, buying copies or seeking permission are guilty of stealing.

It is tempting to think that copyright infringements and lawsuits are more or less the exclusive domain of large institutions. Certainly, the public learns about large scale abuses faster than individual abuses.

Obviously, if a company is going to sue someone, it will seek a person or institution that has been guilty of multiple infringements so that larger damages can be won. It simply doesn't make good economic sense to sue someone who will be ordered to pay only a small amount of damages.

Sometimes, though, lawsuits are brought solely to prove a point. A 1983 case, *Marcus v. Rowley*, involved a dispute between two teachers in the same school. One teacher had prepared and copyrighted a 20-page booklet on cake decorating; the second teacher copied approximately half the pages and included them in her own materials. The amount of money involved was negligible; the author had sold fewer than 100 copies at a price of $2. Nonetheless, the court found the second teacher guilty of copyright violation; her use of the other's materials was not "fair."

What is fair use?

Section 107 of the 1976 Copyright Act deals with "fair use" and specifically states that the fair use of copies in teaching "is not an infringement of copyright."

The "sticking point" is what the term "fair use" means. The section lists four factors to be included in any determination of fair use:

- the purpose and character of the use, including whether such use is of a commercial nature or is for nonprofit educational purposes;
- the nature of the copyrighted work;
- the amount and substantiality of the portion used in relation to the copyrighted work as a whole;
- the effect of the use upon the potential market for or value of the copyright work.

Educators should have little or no trouble complying with the "purpose and character of the work" factor. Teachers generally copy materials to aid the educational process. It should be noted, however, that recreational use of copied materials such as video-cassettes or computer games is generally not allowed under the statute.

"The nature of the copyrighted work" factor can prove a bit more problematic than "character and purpose of the work." Who determines what is the nature of the work-the creator and/or copyright holder, the teacher, the judge and/or the jury? Almost any material can be classified as educational in some context; even a cartoon can be found to have some educational purpose if one is willing to look for it. It seems reasonable that, in determining nature, a court would look to the ordinary use of the work and to the author's intent in creating the work.

The "amount and substantiality" of the work copied is especially troublesome in the use of videocassettes and computer programs. Teachers understand that they are not supposed to copy a whole book, but may not understand that copying a television program or a movie onto videotape or copying a computer program for student use can violate the "amount and substantiality" factor.

In the case of *Encyclopedia Britannica v. Crooks,* an educational company engaged in copying commercially available tapes and television programs for teachers, was found to be in violation of the Copyright Act. The company argued that it was providing an educational service for students and teachers who would otherwise be deprived of important educational opportunities. The court rejected the argument.

Teachers may be tempted to think that their small-scale copying acts could not compare with the scope of the activities in this case. In the majority of instances involving single copying, there is no comparison. A relatively new practice, developing libraries of copies, is emerging in some schools. Whether the collections are of print materials or non-print materials, such as videotapes and computer programs, the practice of building collections can easily be subjected to the same scrutiny as the *Encyclopedia* case.

The last of the four factors, "effect on the market," is also difficult to apply in the educational setting. Arguments can be advanced that students would not rent or purchase commercially available items, even if the copies weren't available. It appears, though, that use of an author's work without appropriate payment for the privilege, is a form of economic harm. Good faith generally will not operate as an acceptable defense in educational copyright or infringement cases.

The court, in *Roy v. Columbia Broadcasting System*, stated: "The federal copyright statute protects copyrighted works against mere copying, even when done in good faith and even when not done to obtain a competitive advantage over the owners of the copyright in the infringed works." (p. 1151)

Guidelines

A congressional committee developed "Guidelines for Classroom Copying in Not-for-Profit Educational Institutions," printed in House Report 94-1476, 94th Congress 2d Sess. (1976). Principals should ensure that teachers have access to copies of the guidelines, which are readily available from local libraries, the Copyright Office, and members of Congress. Although these guidelines do not have the force of law that the statute has, judges have used them in deciding cases. Some examples of the guidelines follow.

For poetry, copying of a complete poem of less than 250 words printed on no more than two pages or of an excerpt of 250 words from a longer poem is allowed. For prose, a complete work of less than 2,500 words or an excerpt from a longer work of not more than 1,000 words or 10% of the work is permissible. The guidelines mandate that copying meet this test of *brevity*.

The copying must be *spontaneous*. The teacher must have decided more or less on the spur of the moment to use an item. Spontaneity presumes that a teacher did not have time to secure permission for use from the copyright holder. A teacher who decides in September to use certain materials in December has ample time to seek permission. In such a situation, failure to seek permission means that the spontaneity requirement will not be met.

A last requirement is that the copying must not have a *cumulative effect*. Making copies of poems by one author would have a cumulative effect and would mean that collected works of the author would not be bought.

Similarly, the practice of "librarying" (building a collection of taped television programs, for example) is not permitted. Copying computer programs is never advisable, unless permission to make copies is included in the purchase or rental agreement.

Videotapes may be kept for 45 days only. During the first 10 days, a teacher may use the tape once in a class (although there is a provision for one repetition for legitimate instructional review). For the remaining 35 days teachers may use the tape for evaluative purposes only.

Technology: moral, ethical, and legal challenges

Ten years ago, most educators—and certainly most Catholic educators—had limited access to computer technology. As the millennium approaches it is hard to imagine life without computers and the related technology of the Information Age. Access to volumes of information that would have taken much time to gather a few years ago can now be obtained in a few moments with the aid of a modem and a database. These developments, as wonderful as they are, present challenges for the educator who seeks to act in ways that are morally, ethically and legally correct.

Appropriateness of materials available

Headlines reveal that several young persons have run away from home as a result of propositions received from persons on the Internet. Since there currently is no truly effective means of monitoring and/or censoring material on the Internet and other networks, there is nothing to prevent unsupervised young people from being in electronic conversation with inappropriate persons about sexual matters, drugs, crime, and other less than suitable topics. The growing popularity of "chat rooms" presents a particular ethical/moral dilemma. Since there are no privacy police, people who log into a chat room can write anything they wish to another person "in the room" at the same time. E-mail provides a means for persons with no prior knowledge of each other to share intimate conversation.

"Chat rooms" and E-mail present issues of morality not unlike those presented by television and movies. The television industry polices itself, at least to a degree. For example, one does not generally find prime-time pornography on the major networks. Although adults channels are available on cable TV, parents and other supervisors can purchase devices that allow them to block access to such channels. Hotels and motels allow parents to call the front desk and have access to movie channels blocked in their rooms.

The movie industry provides a rating system that indicates the appropriateness of content for certain age groups. The dearth of PG movies, however, indicates that movies without sex and violence do not generally sell as well as those containing such elements.

With no equivalent monitoring system in place in the world of cyberspace, parents and other educators must maintain constant vigilance. Consumers need to lobby the computer industry to provide some means of evaluating content and limiting access. Some experts recommend the development of computer programs or microchips that will limit the availability of certain services. Voters need to lobby law-makers to develop legislation that will provide protection for young persons. The First Amendment to the Constitution does permit much leeway in terms of expression, but it does not require that children and teenagers be given unlimited access to other persons' self-expression. Adults must stand firm and monitor computer usage by the young people for whom they are responsible.

Conclusion

Principals are responsible for supervision of all aspects of the educational process. If a teacher is charged with copyright violation, it is likely that the principal will be charged as well. Clear policies and careful monitoring of those policies can lessen exposure to liability. As many legal authorities have observed, copyright violation is stealing. It appears, then, that "Thou shalt not steal" remains good law.

Educators may be tempted to believe the oft-quoted lines from *The Merchant of Venice,* "To do a great right, do a little wrong." Ethical, moral, and legal imperatives do not accept such rationalization. Students, rich or poor, have a right to experience the richness of technology. At the same time, they have a right to expect that adults will protect them from harm and will exercise vigilance over technological, as well as other, behaviors. Lastly, educators themselves must be models of integrity and observe the laws that grant authors and other creators the right to the fruits of their labors. Obviously, the Internet and the Information Highway were not part of Jesus's lived experience, but it is important to reflect on how He would want us to meet the challenges they present in today's world. Catholic educators must surely model their behavior on that of Jesus who scrupulously paid the temple tax, rendered Caesar his due, and exhorted landowners to pay workers a generous wage.

For Reflection and Discussion

- Six students have just told you that Student I, who has managed to bypass the lockout, has been logging onto a chatroom and is planning to visit a 40 year old woman he met on the "May/December Romance Hotline." What will you do?

- You are planning a production of *Oklahoma* for March. The licensing fee is very high. A friend of yours has 20 copies of the librettos and scripts. He says the company didn't ask for them back. He offers to give them to you. How will you respond?

CHAPTER FOURTEEN

SCHOOL HANDBOOKS: WHAT SHOULD BE INCLUDED? HOW BINDING ARE THEY?

Minimum components of faculty handbooks

Parent/student handbooks

Right to amend

How binding are handbooks?

For Reflection and Discussion

CHAPTER FOURTEEN

SCHOOL HANDBOOKS: WHAT SHOULD BE INCLUDED? HOW BINDING ARE THEY?

After the first weeks of school, administrators and students may give a sigh of relief that the opening went well, and the business of Catholic education is moving forward. Now, before the memories fade, is the time to evaluate beginning of the year events and documents. No documents are more important than the faculty and parent/student handbooks, which courts can consider to be legally binding.

Principals, teachers, and parents may ask why a certain item is not covered by a handbook policy or procedure or may state that what is written in a handbook does not seem sufficient for situations that arise. These are important observations and they need to be captured and recorded when made, not six months later when it is time to revise the handbook(s) for the coming school year. Handbook development should be everyone's responsibility, not just the principal's. A principal should consider utilizing a simple index card method for suggested revisions. Anyone who has a suggestion for inclusion or deletion in handbook(s) should note that suggestion on an index card. Only one suggestion per card is allowed. In the spring when handbooks are usually revised or updated, the administrator can sort cards by topic. Then, the administrator or handbook committee can consider each idea. Such an approach makes revision much easier, and does not result in frantic efforts to recall what people said at previous faculty or other meetings.

Minimum components of faculty handbooks

There are six minimum topic areas that should be included in any faculty handbook:

(1) the philosophy of the school,
(2) a list and explanation of teaching duties, including a working definition of what constitutes good teaching,
(3) a list and explanation of non-teaching duties, the policy and procedures for administrative supervision and evaluation of teachers,
(5) a list and explanation of personnel policies, and
(6) sample forms.

These six areas are by no means exhaustive, but they provide a broad, legally solid framework. Almost everything that an administrator would want to include in a handbook can "fit" into one of these categories. For example, a policy on the law relating to child abuse reporting, is a non-teaching duty. A policy that reflects an awareness of students with special needs in classrooms can be placed under the category of teaching duties.

Parent/student handbooks

Parent/student handbooks are, in the opinion of this author, preferable to having simply a student handbook or two separate handbooks. The parents are the parties that contract with the school. Parents pay tuition or support the school in other ways in lieu of tuition, and, in enrolling their child(ren) in school, they are agreeing that both they and their child(ren) will abide by the rules and regulations of the school.

The parent/student handbook should include policies and procedures in the following areas:

(1) Philosophy,
(2) Admission Policies/Notice of Non-Discrimination
(3) Academic Policies,
(4) Communication—how does the parent communicate with teachers and administrators? How do teachers and ad-

ministrators communicate with parents?

(5) Discipline Code, including rules, regulations, penalties, and exceptions,

(6) Extra-curricular Activities, including policies on participation and exclusion from activities,

(7) Parent/Student's Signed Agreement to be bound by the handbook.

Such an agreement, which should be on a detachable card or a separate sheet, can state the following or similar words:

"We, the parent (s) of _____, agree to be governed by this school handbook for the school year _____. We recognize the right and responsibility of the school to make rules and enforce them."

An administrator may also wish to have the student(s) sign, but it must be clearly understood that student(s), unless over the age of eighteen and functioning as adults, cannot legally be held responsible for meeting the terms of a contract.

Right to amend

Since situations can arise that were not foreseen at the time of writing a handbook, the principal should always reserve the right to amend the handbook. Parents and students should be promptly notified of any amendments.

How binding are handbooks?

A sizable number of court cases hold that handbooks can be legally binding, in the same way as other contracting documents are. Some administrators have inserted disclaimers into handbooks stating that they are not legally binding contracts. There are ethical issues that should be considered before administrators publish a handbook to which faculty or parents or students are bound, but which the administrator does not consider as binding the school or its administration. Since courts generally resolve any ambiguity in favor of the person who did not construct the document, it is easy to see how problems can arise. The wise administrator will always attempt to balance ethical and legal issues in decision-making. The wise teacher will share responsibility for handbook development and implementation.

For Reflection and Discussion

- What items in your present parent/student and/or faculty handbooks raise legal issues for you?

- Name and explain two policies, rules, or regulations you would like to see added or revised in current handbooks.

- A student comes into your class with lavender spiked hair, two nose rings, and five pierced earring in each ear. You gently state that she needs to see the vice-principal to determine the appropriateness of her appearance. As she leaves she says, "But the handbook doesn't say I can't have purple-spiked hair, nose rings, or lots of earrings." Other students agree and one asks, "How can you make us do something that is not in the handbook?" How will you reply?

CHAPTER FIFTEEN

CATHOLIC SCHOOLS AND FINANCE: HOW DOES THE LAW APPLY?

Contract law: The basis for Catholic school finances

Tuition contracts

Fees and fundraising

Designated donations

Withholding transcripts for non-payment of tuition

Bonding persons who handle finances

For Reflection and Discussion

CHAPTER FIFTEEN

CATHOLIC SCHOOLS AND FINANCE: HOW DOES THE LAW APPLY?

erhaps no aspect of Catholic school administration is more troublesome than financial matters. Presidents and principals spend much of their time budgeting, collecting tuition, attempting to raise money, and worrying about money. But administrators' fiscal responsibilities extend well beyond balancing budgets and paying bills. Civil law must also be considered when fiscal policies are developed and implemented.

Contract law: The basis for Catholic school finances

Contract law governs the operation of the Catholic school. Persons in Catholic schools surrender their constitutional protections, as it were, when they enter the Catholic school. These persons are not left without protection; their rights are determined by the provisions of the contract they have with the school. Both parents, teachers, and administrators must look to the contracting documents to determine the financial obligations of each party.

Since the school and those who set policy for the school determine the content of contracts, the school's chief administrator should ensure that contracts clearly state financial expectations.

Examples of contract content include the amount of tuition charged, the possible payment arrangements and the penalties for delayed payments. Carefully written documents that leave little, if any, room for disagreement as to their meaning, are administrators' best protection against allegations of unfairness and/or civil lawsuits.

Administrators should ensure that the provisions of the contract are legal. Some Catholic schools have attempted to require parents to work at bingo games or Las Vegas nights as a condition of enrollment. The laws of most states do not permit organizations to use *non-voluntary* workers in operations that state law considers to be gambling. Catholic schools can require service of parents, and that service can be given in weekly bingo games or church festivals or selling raffle tickets or in some other way; however, schools generally are not free to mandate that everyone will work, for example, at three bingo games a year or for six hours at the school festival. In states where bingo and other such games have been legalized, the state regulates the operation and usually requires that those who work at the games be volunteers.

Tuition contracts

Many schools are now requiring parents to sign separate tuition contracts or are including all financial policies in the parent / student handbook. Tuition contracts provide evidence that a debt is owed to the school. In the 1987 case of *Thomas Jefferson School v. Kapros*, the court held that a school could expel a student according to its rules and that the parent could be required to pay the full year's tuition, since he had signed a contract which bound him to the payment of liquidated damages if his child did not complete the school year. Such a judgment may seem harsh, at first glance. Administrators, however, budget for expenses based on a certain number of students; if students withdraw, the expenses remain. As difficult as it may be, those responsible for Catholic schools must remember that the school, while primarily a ministry, is also a business and bills must be paid. When purchasing an automobile, the buyer agrees to make monthly payments; if the person later decides the automobile isn't suitable, he or she is still bound to make the payments to the financier.

Presidents and principals and other policy makers should bear in mind that exceptions can always be made to a policy. For example, if a parent signs a tuition contract and is later transferred to another city, the administrator should be able to make an exception and waive the payment of the remainder of the tuition. If however, a student decides he or she would rather go to a different school, the administrator may decide to hold the parents to the contract.

Fees and fundraising

Presidents, principals, and boards should give serious consideration to developing a policy governing fees, particularly in the area of refunds. The wisest course might be to state that all fees are non-refundable; the administrator could retain the right to make exceptions when appropriate.

Fundraising is a fact of life in Catholic schools. Administrators should ensure that parents and students understand what is expected of them in this regard. The parent/student handbook is a good place for this information.

Designated donations

A not uncommon situation can arise in which an individual proposes to give, for example, the equivalent of a scholarship cash donation to a school, so long as a specific relative or other individual receives the scholarship. If such a gift is accepted, the individual may claim it on his or her income tax return. Such an action is illegal. If a person is getting something for a "donation" the money is not a donation. The IRS takes such situations very seriously, and administrators who knowingly or naively, accept such contributions and certify them as donations put the tax-exempt status of their institutions at risk. In effect, to allow such a donation amounts to aiding and abetting income tax evasion.

Withholding transcripts for non-payment of tuition

When a parent fails to pay tuition and subsequently withdraws a student and requests a transcript, what is an administrator to do? State law can vary. For example, many states allow administrators to withhold transcripts for all educational programs, from elementary through graduate school. Some states require the release of transcripts. For example, Massachusetts state 71, s 34 a states: " Any person operating or maintaining an educational institution within the commonwealth shall, upon request of any student or former student thereof, furnish him a written transcript of his record as a student." If one administers a school in Massachusetts, one must comply.

Even in states without Massachusetts-like laws, there can be liability for failure to issue a transcript. There is developing case law which suggests that if a school continues to provide services to a student whose tuition is in arrears, the school has breached its duty to mitigate damages, and owes a duty to the student, a third party beneficiary, to release a transcript. One possible way to avoid such a situation is to have a policy which does not allow the student to take mid-term or final exams until the tuition is paid. If a transcript is released, it will contain grades of "incomplete". Administrators should consult with school or diocesan attorneys on their state law before attempting to implement such a policy. The law is in a constant state of flux, and this area of transcripts is one of the most challenging.

Bonding persons who handle finances

School administrators should give serious consideration to bonding individuals who handle money for the school. Should an unfortunate situation occur and money be embezzled or otherwise misappropriated, the school will be able to recover lost funds.

The topic of finances is a serious one. Careful planning, consultation with diocesan and/or school attorneys, and periodic review should help the school and those who are responsible for it to keep it functioning in a financially and legally sound manner.

For Reflection and Discussion

- A parent approaches you, a teacher, and asks for your help in convincing the principal that he or she is an honest person and will pay the tuition owed so that his or her child can take exams. Confidentially, the parent tells you that the tuition will probably never be paid, and the child will withdraw after grades are issued. What will you do with this information? How will you answer the parent?

GLOSSARY
OF TERMS

Common Law
Common law is that law not created by a legislature. It includes principles of action based on long-established standards of reasonable conduct and on court judgments affirming such standards. It is sometime called "judge-made law."

Compelling State Interest
Compelling state interest is the overwhelming or serious need for governmental action. The government is said to have a compelling state interest in anti-discrimination legislation and in the elimination of unequal treatment of citizens.

Contract
A contract is an agreement between two parties. The essentials of a contract are: (1) mutual assent (2) by legally competent parties (3) for consideration (4) to subject matter that is legal and (5) in a form of agreement that is legal.

Defamation
Defamation is an unprivileged communication. It can be either spoken (slander) or written (libel).

Due Process (constitutional)
Due process is fundamental fairness under the law. There are two types:
- Substantive Due Process: The constitutional guarantee that no person shall be arbitrarily deprived of his life, liberty, or property; the essence of substantive due process is protection from arbitrary unreasonable action" (Black). Substantive due process concerns what is done as distinguished from *how* it is done (procedural due process).

- Procedural Due Process: how the process of depriving someone of something is carried out; *how it is done*. The minimum requirements of constitutional due process are notice and a *hearing* before an *impartial tribunal*.

Foreseeability

Foreseeability is the "the reasonable anticipation that harm or injury is the likely result of acts or omission" (Black). It is not necessary that a person anticipate the particular injury that might result from an action, but only that danger or harm in general might result.

Negligence

Negligence is the absence of the degree of care which a reasonable person would be expected to use in a given situation. Legal negligence requires the presence of four elements: duty, violation of duty, proximate cause, and injury.

Policy

A policy is a guide for discretionary action. Policy states what is to be done, not *how* it is to be done.

Proximate Cause

Proximate cause is a contributing factor to an injury. The injury was the result of or reasonably foreseeable outcome of the action or inaction said to be the proximate cause.

State Action

State action is the presence of the government in an activity to such a degree that the activity may be considered to be that of the government.

Tort

A tort is a civil or private wrong as distinguished from a crime.

BIBLIOGRAPHY

Americans with Disabilities Act (1992).

Agostini v. Felton, 117 S. Ct 1997 (1997).

Aguilar v. Felton, 105 S.Ct. 3232 (1985).

Benitez v. NYC B.O.E. 543, N.Y.2d 29 (1989).

Black, Henry Campell. *Black's law dictionary* (6th ed.) St. Paul: West, 1990).

Bonnie Ann F. by John R.V. Callalen I.S.D. , S.D. Tex., Civ. No. C-91-259 (1993).

Brooks v. Logan and Joint District No. 2 (1995).

The Buckley Amendment of 1975.

Civil Rights Act of 1964.

Copyright Act of 1909.

Copyright Act of 1976.

Doe by and through Doe v. BOE of Tullahoma City Schools, C.A. Tenn., No. 92-5996 (1993).

Jane Doe v. Spec. Sch. Dis. of St. Louis County, 901 F.2d 642 (8th Cir. 1990).

D.T. et al v. Ind. Sch. Dis. No. 16 of Pawnee City, 894 F.2d 1176 (1980).

Encyclopedia Brittanica v. Crooks, 542 F. Supp. 1156 (W.D.N.Y. 1982).

Franklin v. Gwinnet County Public Schools (1992).

Geraci v. St. Xavier High School, 12 Ohio Op. 3d 146 (Ohio, 1978).

"Guidelines for Classroom Copying in Not-for-Profit Educational Institutions", House Report 94-1476, 94th Congress 2d Session (1976).

Individuals with Disabilities Education Act (IDEA) Amendments (1997).

Levandowski v. Jackson City School District, 328 S.2d 339 (Minn. 1976).

Marcus v. Rowley, 695 F.2d 1171 (1983).

Medlin v. Bass, 327 N.C. 587, 398 S.E. 2d 460 (1990).

Merickel, *The Educator's Right to Fair Use of Copyrighted Works,* 51 Ed.Law.Rpr. 711, (1989).

New Jersey v. T.L.O., 105 S. Ct. 733 (1985).

Pastoral Statement of U.S. Catholic Bishops on Handicapped People (1988).

The People v. Ralph Gamez, 235 Cal.App.3d 957 (1991).

Public Law 94-142: The Individuals with Disabilities Education Act (1975; Reauthorized, 1990).

Rehabilitation Act of 1973.

Rendell-Baker v. Kohn, 102 S.Ct. 2764 (1982).

Roy v. Columbia Broadcasting System, 503 F.Supp.1137 (S.D.N.Y. 1980).

Short v. Griffits 255 S.W. 2d 479 (V.A., 1979)

Smith v. Archbishop of St. Louis, 632 S.W.2d 516 (1982).

Stehn v. MacFadden Foundations, 434 F.2d 811 (U.S.C.A. 6th Cir., 1970).

Thomas Jefferson School v. Kapros, 728 S.W. 2d 315 (1987).

Tinker v. Des Moines Independent Community School District et al., 393 U.S. 503 (1969).

Titus v. Lindberg, 228 A.2d 65 (N.J., 1967).

Zobrest v. Catalina Foothills School District, 113 S. Ct. 2462 (1993).

ABOUT THE
AUTHOR

S r. Mary Angela Shaughnessy is a Sister
of Charity of Nazareth who has taught at all levels of Catholic
education from elementary through graduate school. Sr. Mary
Angela holds a B.A. in English, M.A.s in English and Education, a
J.D. in Law, and a Ph.D. in Educational Administration and Supervision. Her research centers on the law as it affects Catholic education and Church ministry. She is the author of fifteen texts on
law and Catholic schools.

Sr. Mary Angela is a regular speaker at the NCEA Conventions
and has served as adjunct professor in various university programs, including a stint as Visiting Professor at the University of
San Francisco since 1988. Currently, Sr. Mary Angela is Univer-

sity Legal Counsel and Professor of Edu-
cation at Spalding University in Louisville,
Kentucky, and serves as a consultant to
numerous dioceses across the country.
She is a member of the bar in the state of
Kentucky.

She is the recipient of numerous
awards, including the NCEA Secondary
Schools Department Award. Most re-
cently, she was named one of the 25 most
influential persons in Catholic education
over the last 25 years.